CONSUMER GUIDE®

CHEVROLET
1955-1957

PUBLICATIONS INTERNATIONAL, LTD.

Contents

Louis Weber, C.E.O.
Publications International, Ltd.
7373 North Cicero Avenue
Lincolnwood, Illinois 60646

Permission is never granted for commercial
purposes.

Manufactured in the U.S.A.

8 7 6 5 4 3 2 1

ISBN 1-56173-311-3

1956   1957

"THE HOT ONE'S EVEN HOTTER!"

PAGE THIRTY-EIGHT

After a rousing 1955, fans might have wondered what Chevrolet would do for 1956. They needn't have worried, for there would be more style (bigger and more "important" looking), more power, and more refinements—all geared "to make the going sweeter."

THE ULTIMATE "CLASSIC" CHEVY

PAGE SIXTY-SIX

Chevy touted its '57 as "Sweet, Smooth, and Sassy!" And indeed, the new styling *was* sweet, the finest of the 1955-57 "classic" Chevys; the new Turboglide transmission was "as smooth as velvet underpants"; and the new fuel-injected 283 V-8 was *very* sassy!

Photo Credits:

Orazio Aiello: 20 (bottom), 31 (top), 53 (top), 73, 96; **Sam Griffith:** 4, 7 (bottom), 9, 12 (top), 13, 20 (top), 21, 24-25, 35 (bottom), 36-37, 39, 60-61, 65, 74, 79, 82-83 (bottom), 84-85 (top), 94-95; **Jerry Heasley:** 52, 90; **Fergus Hernandes:** 14, 15, 67, 70 (top); **Bud Juneau:** 6 (top), 58-59 (top); **Dan Lyons:** 28-29, 30-31, 32-33, 43 (bottom), 62, 63; **Vince Manocchi:** 7 (top), 12 (middle), 70 (middle); **Doug Mitchel:** 7 (middle), 22-23, 44-45, 46-47, 53 (middle, bottom), 57, 76-77; **Mike Mueller:** 48-49, 86-87; **Ned Schreiner:** 92; **Bob Tenney:** 12 (bottom); **Nicky Wright:** 6 (bottom), 27, 43 (top), 56, 70 (bottom), 72, 88-89.

Acknowledgements:

Special thanks to: Charles M. Jordan, Vice President, General Motors Design Staff; Floyd Joliet, Administrative Operations, General Motors Design Staff; Kari St. Antoine, Chevrolet Public Relations; Bill Bodnarchuk; Ron Pittman; Jim Cahill.

1911-1954

FROM OBSCURITY TO "USA-1"

Henry Ford may have put America on wheels, but during the late '30s and '40s it was a Chevrolet that most buyers chose. By World War II Chevrolet was well entrenched as "USA-1." Dull but dependable, it appealed to millions because of its low price, practicality, and pleasant styling.

"Baseball, hot dogs, apple pie, and Chevrolet." This is just one of the advertising lines Chevy has used over the years, and the statement is just as American in feel and spirit as the Chevrolet automobile has traditionally been. And really, none of the Chevys over the past 80 years has been closer to "The heartbeat of America," to borrow a current Chevy advertising tagline, than the so-called "classic" Chevys of 1955-57. America has been in love with them for three and a half decades now. Why? Nostalgia, certainly, plus sheer numbers: nearly five million built during those three short years. As one writer so accurately put it: "Just about everybody had one once."

But there's much more to it than that. Like other "great" cars, Chevrolet's 1955-57 passenger models don't just mirror their time—they transcend it. In the process, they retain an undeniable magic for those who knew them when, yet beckon to younger enthusiasts not yet born when the last one rolled off the assembly line.

An earlier generation of enthusiasts was quick to acclaim these cars "classic," a term once reserved only for certain prewar rarities in the luxury class, as determined by the Classic Car Club of America. But the term is nonetheless appropriate in its own way for the Chevys, because though far more numerous, they're just as significant and memorable. They forever erased the "old fogey" image of General Motors' volume make, introduced a landmark V-8 that set a new standard of performance value, and left us with some of the sweetest, cleanest styling in postwar history. No wonder Chevy sold so many.

Such intrinsic goodness partly explains their broad, devoted following, rare among mass-production models of any era. Only those history-making prewar Fords—Model T, Model A, and the 1932 V-8—have inspired such enduring, widespread admiration. But while their fans are dwindling now, the Chevys seem to have more than ever. That's why you still see so many 1955-57s today, each a "solid gold" treasure to its lucky owner.

Yet it's important to remember that Chevrolet didn't set out to produce a classic, merely what one critic termed "an average automobile that offered good dollar value, was enjoyable to drive, easy to maintain, and economical to operate. Certainly the high-performance editions were intended to strike a responsive chord in the hearts of horsepower aficionados, but the bread-and-butter models were built with Mr. Joe Average in mind."

Of course, Chevrolet had prospered with nothing *but* bread-and-butter cars since the early Twenties. Well before World War II it was GM's largest-volume division, had helped its parent achieve near total market dominance, and was more or less established as "USA-1," the nation's most popular make. Chevy first took that title from its archrival in 1927 during Ford's changeover from the Model T to the Model A, and by the late Thirties was firmly in command in terms of sales and production. The GM division's success rested on cars and trucks that one author characterized as "reasonably priced, reliable, easy to repair, easy to resell," offering "the masses a solid formula of value, comfort, and dependability backed by the strongest, largest, and wealthiest dealer network in the world."

Chevrolet's history traces back to 1911, when the Classic Six was announced, although production didn't get underway until 1912. First-year output was recorded as a modest 2999 units. Developed by Louis Chevrolet, former race car driver and mechanical whiz, it was an upmarket car that sold for $2250, $450 *more* than a Cadillac touring car. More than anyone, however—including Louis Chevrolet—it was wheeler-dealer and ex-GM president and founder William Crapo Durant who put Chevrolet on the map. Durant had founded GM in 1908, but he lost control in 1910 and moved on in 1911. Almost immediately he began plotting to create another automotive empire, and it was Chevrolet that was to be its cornerstone. Durant and Chevrolet didn't see eye to eye, however, the former wanting a low-priced mainstream car, the latter a finer, bigger automobile worthy of his name. Chevrolet walked away from the Chevy operation in 1913, leaving Durant free to mold the car however he chose.

Offering a lower-medium-priced line, the Chevy was moderately successful, but in 1915 the 490 debuted, the number reflecting the price and Durant's desire to challenge Henry Ford head-on. At the time Henry was selling his Model T for $490, but Durant's move inspired Ford to respond by lowering the price to $440. In any case, Chevrolet sold well enough—and its stock was strong enough—to help Durant manipulate control of a majority of GM stock, and thus regain the GM presidency in June 1916. Chevrolet was officially folded into GM in 1918, and its fortunes have been tied to GM's ever since. Unfortunately for Durant, his wheelings and dealings were destined to catch up with him again, and

he was forced out of GM for the final time in late 1920.

The mutual, rapid growth of GM and Chevy in the Twenties and Thirties stemmed largely from president and board chairman Alfred P. Sloan, the revolutionary business practices he brought to GM (and thus Chevy), and the astute designers, engineers, and managers he attracted. Among the last was William S. "Big Bill" Knudsen, who became Chevrolet general manager in 1922—ironically, after leaving Ford after a major disagreement with old Henry. Knudsen quickly set about transforming a cheap car of dubious reliability into a rugged, yet still affordable, car of genuine quality. Knudsen also went after Ford sales "one for one" through a vastly expanded dealer body and countless production improvements. Gradually, notes one historian, "Chevy closed the gap [with Ford's] legendary Model T by offering bigger, faster, brighter, and altogether superior cars for just a little more money."

And it didn't stop there. In 1929, two years after Ford began tooling the Tin Lizzie's long-overdue successor, Chevy became a "Six at the Price of Four" by switching to the overhead-valve engine, since lovingly enshrined as the "Stovebolt," because of its large, quarter-inch slotted head bolts. Also sometimes known affectionately as the "Cast-Iron Wonder," it grew from 194 cubic inches and 50 horsepower to 216.5 cid and 85 bhp by 1937, when it was strengthened and completely redesigned. After adding five bhp for '41, it continued unchanged until 1950 as Chevy's sole powerplant. Aside from stout-hearted simplicity that would carry it all the way through 1962, the Stovebolt was important for prompting Henry Ford to respond with the industry's first low-price V-8. But even that couldn't halt the momentum, and by the time Knudsen replaced Sloan as GM president in 1937, Chevy was indeed USA-1.

Several other features contributed to Chevrolet's prewar success: "Knee Action" independent front suspension (initially troublesome, like the Stovebolt, but just as quickly improved), clashless synchromesh transmission, all-steel "Turret-Top" body construction, and hydraulic brakes. Chevy also benefited from GM's early emphasis on design, which emerged in the Thirties as a new and often decisive sales factor. Credit Harley J. Earl, who established the first in-house styling department at a major automaker, GM's famous Art & Colour Section, which he would head for three decades. His influence at Chevy was evident as early as 1930. "We can't afford big mistakes," he said later, "and we don't even like little ones." Thus, Chevy styling wasn't always adventuresome, but it was always salable, unlike that of some rivals. And occasionally, it was brilliant: the Cadillac-inspired 1932 Eagle series and the smooth, Buick-like '41s were good-looking cars by any standard, the peak of prewar Chevy design.

Chevrolet continued its winning ways in the decade that both preceded and shaped its mid-Fifties "classics." Like other makes, its 1946 models were little more than warmed-over '42s, which had evolved from the popular '41s, but the huge postwar seller's market took every one. Additional minor facelifts followed for 1947-48, by which time volume was back up to nearly 700,000 units for model year '48, despite the early postwar material shortages and strikes at both GM and its suppliers.

Concurrently, the division weathered two unexpected leadership changes. First, general manager Marvin E. Coyle was replaced in June 1946 by Nicholas E. Dreystadt, his counterpart at Cadillac. Then Dreystadt was felled by cancer in August 1948, and his successor, William F. Armstrong, resigned because of illness after only a year. That brought Thomas H. Keating to the helm in 1949, the historic year when the U.S. auto industry completed its postwar design overhaul.

In line with GM's restyle, begun the previous season at Cadillac and Oldsmobile, the '49 Chevrolets were smoother, lower, and longer-looking, though their 115-inch wheelbase was actually an inch shorter than in 1941-48. Featured were flush front fenders, closer-fitting rear fenders, broader grilles, curved windshields, and more integrated body lines. Models expanded with racy new Fleetline two- and four-door fastback sedans in Special and costlier DeLuxe trim. The Styleline Special series listed two-door Town Sedan, four-door Sport Sedan, Sport Coupe, and business coupe, all notchbacks. Styleline DeLuxe deleted the last but added the customary convertible and two four-door wagons—one with structural wood, Chevy's last woody, and a look-alike all-steel job, the make's first.

Yet for all their new finery, the '49s were still the same mundane people-movers Chevys had always been: as dull as the engine that powered them. Though it was called "Blue Flame," the old six was still spinning out 90 bhp at 3300 rpm, while the chassis hadn't changed much since the

Knee-Action days. Ford, meanwhile, wrapped its equally aged flathead V-8 in contemporary slab-sided styling and adopted a completely modern suspension, thus polishing its long-time image as the "performance" car of the low-price field.

So while buyers liked the '49 Chevys, more of them liked that year's Ford, which admittedly benefited from an early sendoff in June 1948. But though Dearborn won the model year production race by more than 117,000 units, Chevy took calendar year honors by almost 269,000 cars with a record total of just over 1.1 million, better than 40 percent up on 1948, remarkable in view of the stronger competition.

Chevy extended its lead for 1950 with two trendsetting "firsts" for the low-price field that would prove immensely popular: the Bel Air hardtop-convertible in the Styleline DeLuxe series, and optional two-speed Powerglide automatic transmission. Accompanying the latter was a 235.5-cid six with 105 bhp, while the existing 216.5-cid engine somehow gained two extra horses to 92. Styling stayed mostly the same, and Bendix "Jumbo-Drum" brakes arrived. With all this, Chevy built around 1.5-million cars for both the

The 1949 and '50 Chevrolets: $1508 Styleline DeLuxe Sport Coupe (*top*, owner: Sam Turner) and the $1847 Styleline DeLuxe convertible (*above*, owner: William E. Goodsene)

calendar and model years, besting Ford's market share 22.8 to 17.8 percent.

The following year saw industry-wide production cutbacks prompted by material shortages due to the Korean conflict. Ford answered Chevy's 1950 exclusives, while USA-1 made do with a mild—though pleasing—facelift. Both rivals lost market share, but Chevy managed to widen its margin, 20.9 to 16.9 percent.

The '52 spread was 17.9 percent for Ford, 20.2 for Chevy, and Ford would likely have made bigger inroads had there not been government-mandated production restrictions on all auto companies. The reason Ford might have improved was that it was completely redesigned that year, the second time since the war, while Chevy had but another facelift, and an extremely modest one at that. Had GM dropped the ball? Apparently so. In an age when buyers expected "all-new" looks and more horsepower almost annually, Chevrolet was still offering reasonably stylish but staid cars that didn't change much from year to year. Lamented one Chevy exec: "Every time a prospective buyer saw one, he thought of his grandmother."

But GM had already recognized the problem. In December 1951 its Engineering Policy Committee had decided it had better "turn Chevrolet around" before it was too late. Given the industry's then-customary three-year lead times, this decision wouldn't reach full fruition until 1955. However, several interim developments suggested that USA-1 was about to undergo a second transformation.

The result appeared for 1953 as the most changed Chevys since 1949. Stylist Carl Renner dressed up the old '49 bodies with fresh sheetmetal below the belt and revised C-pillar window designs on most models (particularly the Bel Air hardtop), while divided windshields gave way to one-piece glass. Fastback sedans were canceled due to declining sales, and the lineup was reordered into low-price One-Fifty, mid-range Two-Ten, and top-line Bel Air series. The smaller six was scrapped, and higher compression boosted the 235 to 105 bhp with stickshift (7.1:1) or 115 with Powerglide (7.7:1). The latter was also aided by new aluminum pistons (replacing cast iron) and insert-type rod bearings plus a more modern, pressurized lubrication system. Manual-transmission engines would get these changes for '54. All this reflected the presence of new chief engineer Edward N. Cole, who arrived in May 1952 from Cadillac, where he'd teamed with motor master Harry F. Barr on that division's milestone, high-compression, overhead-valve V-8 of 1949.

But the most visible symbol of Chevy's vibrant metamorphosis was the Corvette roadster, the 1953 Motorama "dream car" that went into very limited production late that year. Boasting a 150-bhp six with triple carburetors and 8.0:1 compression, the sleek, fiberglass-bodied two-seater left no one thinking of grandmother, and the excitement it spread over the regular Chevy line was like nothing the division had ever seen—just what the sales force wanted.

It was also what they needed. Determined to regain sales supremacy, Ford launched an all-out production "blitz" in 1953 as the industry shifted back into high gear with the end of the production restrictions brought on by the Korean conflict. Forced to sell cars they hadn't ordered, Ford dealers resorted to heavy discounting. Chevy had no choice but to follow suit, and the race was on. By 1954, the resulting buyer's market found Chrysler Corporation reeling and the independent producers moribund as Chevy and Ford publicly argued over sales figures. The market share gap was smaller than ever: 25.7 percent for Chevy, 25.3 percent for Ford.

Their '54 products were as closely matched. Though both wore only modest facelifts, Ford retired its old flathead V-8 in favor of a fine new overhead-valve "Y-block" engine, arriving with 239 cid and a modest 130 horsepower. Also adopted was ball-joint front suspension. Chevy replied with more chrome and a fortified Blue Flame packing 115 bhp with stickshift (same as that year's 223 Ford six) or 125 with Powerglide. Model choices expanded with a Two-Ten Del Ray club coupe (a spiffy two-door with a vinyl interior) and a four-door Bel Air Townsman wagon, which joined the carryover One-Fifty and Two-Ten Handyman models. Also returning from '53 were two- and four-door sedans in each series, One-Fifty utility sedan, and the Bel Air convertible and Sport Coupe hardtop. Meanwhile, the Two-Ten Sport Coupe and ragtop were dropped, as was the One-Ten club coupe. New options included power brakes and power front seat and windows.

Despite its recent lack of product pizzazz and Ford's hard press, Chevrolet had somehow remained USA-1. Now its all-new '55s were ready, and they couldn't have been better timed. Another history-making year was in the offing, and the first of the "classic" Chevys were ready to set Detroit on its ear. A national love affair was about to begin.

Chevy boasted a modest facelift for 1951; the Fleetline DeLuxe two-door (*top*) listed at $1629. (Owner: Bob Hassinger) The 1953 and '54 Bel Air four-door sedans (*center and bottom*): $1874 and $1884. (Owners: Charles Van der Velde and William and Joseph Schoenbeck)

1955

"THE HOT ONE" ARRIVES

Chevrolet's *red-hot* hill-flatteners!
162 H.P. V8 · 180 H.P. V8

Chevrolet shed its stodgy old image in 1955, replacing it with all-new "Motoramic" styling and two "silk-and-dynamite" V-8s. So impressive were the new Chevys that they are now often referred to as "classics."

Don't argue with *this* baby!" warned one Chevrolet ad in 1955. Indeed, Chevy did have a lot to crow about that year, and it knew it. GM's largest and most successful division wasn't the least bit bashful about broadcasting the news about its all-new 1955 lineup. And Chevy wasn't wrong, either, for it can be convincingly argued that the '55 Chevy was one of those happy—and rare—cars whose whole exceeded the sum of its parts.

Completely redesigned, with pretty styling and the option of a potent new "Turbo-Fire" V-8, it was not just the most changed Chevy since the war, but the most exciting car ever to wear the bowtie badge. The sales brochure summed it up best: "New Look! New Life! New Everything!" Terry V. Boyce agreed; in his book *Chevy V-8s*, he proclaimed the '55 Chevy "The most changed new car of the Fifties." Some ads, meanwhile, concentrated on the handsome '55 design, describing it as "'Show Car' Styling at its Beautiful Best!"

Life magazine agreed. In September 1983, it did a feature on "The 10 Best & 10 Worst American Cars," this partly in honor of General Motors' 75th Anniversary. Chevys appeared on both lists, the sad-sack subcompact Vega of the Seventies being the second worst, with the flamboyant '59 "batwing" coming in fifth on the same list. On the other hand, the '55 Chevy Bel Air was on the "10 Best" list—and rightly so—as the "Wheels that mesmerized the *Grease* generation."

This accolade was well deserved, for the public loved—and still loves—the 1955 Chevy, and the same-generation '56s and '57s as well. The acceptance of the all-new and radical '55 wasn't automatic by any means, however, but the time was right as 1955 was a magic year sales-wise for the entire industry. The car was right, too, with styling and engineering so outstanding that in retrospect it's hard to understand that Chevy was taking a chance in undertaking such a massive image-changing overhaul. In 1955, Chevrolet alone accounted for 1.7 million cars out of a total 7.1 million produced in the U.S. That was an industry record that would stand until 1963, and Chevy's share of the pie was nearly 24 percent, and fully 45 percent of the low-price market. Most every make did well that season, of course, because most were "all-new" or nearly new, and Chevy's revitalized Ford and Plymouth rivals also tallied production gains of some 400,000 units over 1954. Yet more than 30 years later, it's the Chevy that's remembered best.

This timelessness derives from a basic design integrity unusual among mass-market Detroiters, which tend to be compromises hashed out with one eye on the sales charts and the other on the bottom line. Not that a great many designers and engineers didn't have a hand in the '55 Chevy. But as one writer observed: "It definitely wasn't a car by committee. One man shepherded the ['55] through all its many stages, from first pencil line to running automobile. And that man was Edward Nicholas Cole."

Chevrolet had just started on its '55s when GM president Charles E. Wilson, future president Harlow H. Curtice, and Louis C. Goad interviewed Cole about becoming Chevy's manufacturing manager. He declined. "I didn't think the product was exciting enough," he said later. But management had just decided to "turn Chevrolet around," so they asked if he'd like to take over from Edward H. "Crankshaft" Kelley as division chief engineer. Cole said he would, if Kelley would step aside. Kelley obliged, becoming manufacturing chief, so Cole set up shop in May 1952.

Soon afterward, GM chairman Alfred P. Sloan asked Cole about his plans for Chevy Engineering. Cole wanted more staff—much more. Sloan agreed, and the department soon ballooned from 850 to 2900 employees. Later, Wilson laughingly told Cole, "I'll bet that's the first time you

This page: As of November 3, 1952, the general shape of the 1955 Chevy was fairly well advanced. The wraparound windshield was already decided upon, as were the contours of the wheel openings. Note the 1954-style taillights. This coupe was dubbed the "Grand Prix," but the limited sales appeal of a three-passenger car prevented it from making it into production. *Opposite page*: The '55 Chevy underwent extensive pre-production testing. The prototype seen here (*top*) has a '53 front end grafted onto the '55 body to disguise it from curious eyes when driven on public roads. Other November 1953 styling studies (*bottom*) show rooflines somewhat akin to those used on the 1953-54 Chevys.

How Chevrolet Design Compared to its Competition

The '55 Chevy (*top*) boasted attractive styling:
a Ferrari-style grille up front, two-toning on the
bodysides, and Cadillac-inspired taillights.
(Owner: Bill Curran) Ford, not to be outdone
(*center*), sported a full-width eggcrate grille,
"Darrin-dip" two-toning, and large round taillights.
(Owner: Alan C. Parker) Plymouth (*bottom*)
was all-new with hooded headlights and a single-bar
grille, fussy two-toning, and large vertical taillights.
(Car courtesy of Community Trading Center)

ever had your plans approved without submitting them."

Cole needed the help. Because an all-new Chevy was more or less assumed by this point, a lot of work would have to be done quickly if he hoped to have it ready for '55. He also knew it would need a V-8 to provide the youthful performance that would transform Chevy's reputation for trustworthy but tepid cars.

As it turned out, Kelley was already working on one, basically a scaled-down, 230-cubic-inch version of the overhead-valve 1949 Cadillac V-8 that Cole had designed with Harry F. Barr. But Cole rejected it as too rich for Chevy's production budget, while an expected lack of power precluded a small V-6 created in 1947 by John Dolza of GM's Central Engineering Staff. There was now little time left for alternatives. With all the development phases involved, Cole would have just 15 weeks to devise his new engine.

So he promptly called his friend Barr, who came over from Cadillac to become assistant chief engineer a month after Cole joined Chevrolet. Together with Kelley, they not only beat the deadline but crafted an engine so good that it's still around today, albeit with numerous modifications made possible only by subsequent technological developments.

How'd they do it? As Cole reflected in 1974: "You just *know* you want five main bearings—there's no decision to make. We knew that a certain bore/stroke relationship was the most compact. We knew we'd like a displacement of 265 cubic inches, and that automatically established the bore and stroke [3.75 x 3.00 inches]. And we never changed any of this. We released our engine for tooling direct from the drawing boards—that's how crazy and confident we were."

Cole's "whole concept" for the '55 Chevy "was built around lighter components," and the new V-8 was no exception. Pushrods, for example, were hollow, and valve guides were integral with the cylinder heads, which were die-cast and completely interchangeable. The intake manifold provided a common water outlet to each. A short stroke meant short connecting rods (just 5.7 inches center distance) and pressed-in piston pins eliminated the need for slitting the rod and a locking bolt. Instead of working off a common shaft, each rocker arm was independent, assembled over a valve stem and pushrod retained by a fulcrum ball and lock nut, so deflection of one rocker wouldn't affect the others. With either mechanical or

hydraulic lifters, the valves were lashed by simply turning the nut. A bonus was reduced reciprocating mass for higher maximum rpm.

Accordingly, Chevy specified three-ring, slipper-type "autothermic" aluminum pistons, with a circumferential expander for the single oil ring providing axial and radial force to control oil burning. Instead of alloy iron, the crankshaft was made of pressed forged steel, and newly developed forging techniques enabled it to be comparatively short for low torsional vibration with no sharp peaks; a harmonic balancer eliminated remaining vibration. Main bearings of equal diameter carried maximum load in their lower halves by omitting the customary oil groove, which reduced wear and doubled capacity. Exhaust manifolds were routed near the top of the heads, the passages flared up and out "ram's horn" style. Ports were fully water-jacketed for better heat dissipation around valve seats.

Chevy saved more weight with novel stamped-metal rocker arms and a splash lubrication system that eliminated separate and costly oil feeder lines. The former, originated by Pontiac engineer Clayton B. Leach, was borrowed from that division's slightly larger new 1955 V-8, which was designed at about the same time and shared Chevy's valvetrain layout. This in turn

Engineering-wise, the big news at Chevrolet for 1955 was its new "Turbo-Fire" V-8 engine. Chevy had built a V-8 briefly in 1917-18, but it was a poor seller and soon dropped. The new one, however, was destined for greatness—a lightweight, high-revving overhead-valve unit producing 162 horsepower with a two-barrel carburetor and single exhaust, or 180 with a four-barrel and duals. Chevy called it a "*red-hot*" hill flattener. (Owner: Bill Curran)

suggested forcing oil up through the hollow pushrods to a hole in the rocker and out onto the top, thus lubricating the ball surface and valve stem. It also eliminated the need for oil passages in the head. Said Barr: "The ball was mounted onto a stud that was pressed into the cylinder head. These were all new ideas, and very good as far as automation was concerned."

Asked whether the Chevy V-8 pioneered any major breakthrough, Cole reflected, "If so, it was when we decided to make the precision cylinder blocks [with] an entirely different casting technique. We used the green-sand core for the valley between the bores . . . to eliminate the dry-sand core so that we could turn the block upside down. We cast it upside down so the plate that holds the bore cores could be accurately located. This way, we could cast down to ⁵⁄₃₂nds jacket walls." Originated by John Dolza with his stillborn V-6, the technique

made for an unheard-of degree of manufacturing precision.

Though only the second V-8 in Chevy history (the first was a short-lived late-Teens engine), the 265 was a landmark: 30 percent more powerful and 40 pounds lighter than the old Stovebolt six, a tribute

to its careful engineering. Named "Turbo-Fire," it arrived with an 8.0:1 compression ratio and a rated 162 horsepower with two-barrel carburetor. A "Power-Pack" version, which Chevy called the "Super Turbo-Fire," was added during the year as an option for all but wagons, with a

The '55 Bel Air hardtop (*above*), called Sport Coupe by Chevy, listed at $2206 with the six, but most came with the optional V-8—note the "V" emblem under the taillight (*opposite page*). The hardtop sported chrome "top bows" inside, mimicking a ragtop, while the Bel Air's "twin-cove" dash featured an appliqué with tiny bowties. (Owner: Jim Van Gondon)

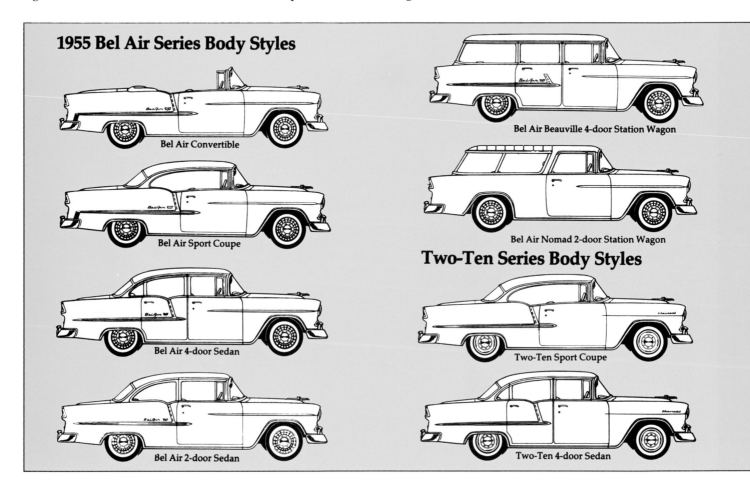

1955 Bel Air Series Body Styles

Bel Air Convertible

Bel Air Sport Coupe

Bel Air 4-door Sedan

Bel Air 2-door Sedan

Bel Air Beauville 4-door Station Wagon

Bel Air Nomad 2-door Station Wagon

Two-Ten Series Body Styles

Two-Ten Sport Coupe

Two-Ten 4-door Sedan

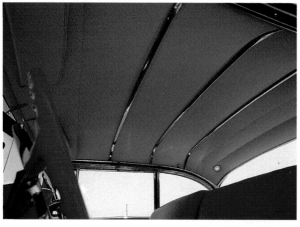

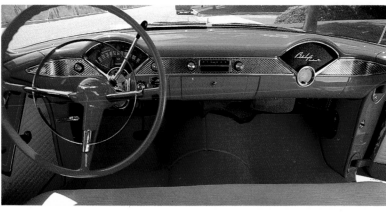

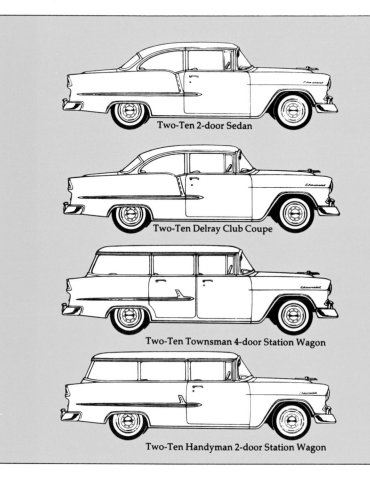

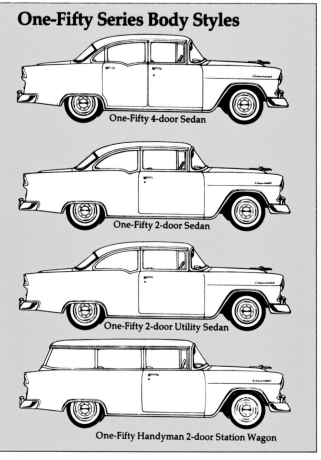

One-Fifty Series Body Styles

Two-Ten 2-door Sedan

Two-Ten Delray Club Coupe

Two-Ten Townsman 4-door Station Wagon

Two-Ten Handyman 2-door Station Wagon

One-Fifty 4-door Sedan

One-Fifty 2-door Sedan

One-Fifty 2-door Utility Sedan

One-Fifty Handyman 2-door Station Wagon

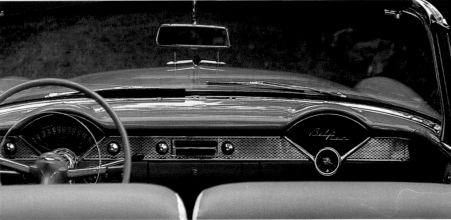

smashing 180 bhp via dual exhausts and a Rochester four-barrel carb. Further, late in the model year Chevy advertised in *Motor Trend* magazine and elsewhere: "**SPECIAL:** Added power for the Chevrolet 'Super Turbo-Fire V-8'—the new 195-h.p. Special Power Kit now available at extra cost on special order." This engine, intended primarily for racing, started as the Power-Pack, to which were installed a Corvette camshaft and valve springs. Meantime, higher compression and minor internal changes brought the venerable Blue Flame six to 123 bhp with stickshift and 136

with automatic, still with a one-barrel carburetor.

Both the six and V-8 could be teamed with one of three transmissions. The standard three-speed column-shift manual pulled a 3.70:1 rear axle, while the extra-cost Borg-Warner overdrive—the unit's first appearance on a GM car—had 4.11:1 gearing. Marketed as "Touch-Down" overdrive, it dropped engine revolutions by 22 percent from 25-30 mph up. The optional two-speed Powerglide automatic returned with a 3.55:1 rear axle.

Besides his V-8 work, Barr supervised

Sportiest of all the '55 Chevrolets was the Bel Air convertible (*both pages*). It was listed at a base price of $2206, or $2305 with the 162-bhp V-8 as on the car seen here. Note the Delco 12-volt battery in the engine compartment—Chevy was a year ahead of Ford and Plymouth in switching over from the old six-volt electrical systems. Inside, the clock was mounted to the right side of the instrument panel, making it hard for the driver to read. The radio speaker was in the same location. The centrally mounted glove box was far more convenient, however. Ragtops featured an all-vinyl interior, nicely two-toned on both the seats and the door panels. (Owner: Archie L. Packard, Jr.)

Exterior Color Selections for the 1955 Chevrolet

1955 COLORS	Bel-Air						Two-Ten						One-Fifty			
	4-door sedan	2-door sedan	Sport Coupe	Convertible	Station Wagon	Nomad	4-door sedan	2-door sedan	Sport Coupe	Delray Club Coupe	2-door Station Wagon	4-door Station Wagon	4-door sedan	2-door sedan	Utility sedan	2-door Station Wagon
SOLID COLORS																
Harvest Gold			●													
Onyx Black	●	●	●	●			●	●		●			●	●	●	
Sea-Mist Green	●	●					●	●		●			●	●	●	●
Neptune Green	●	●	●		●		●	●		●	●	●	●	●	●	●
Skyline Blue	●	●					●	●		●			●	●	●	
Glacier Blue	●	●	●		●		●	●		●	●	●	●	●	●	
Copper Maroon		●	●				●	●					●	●		
Shoreline Beige	●	●	●		●	●	●	●			●	●	●	●	●	
Autumn Bronze							●	●			●	●	●	●	●	●
India Ivory	●	●					●	●		●			●	●	●	
Shadow Gray	●	●					●	●					●	●	●	
Gypsy Red				●												
Regal Turquoise					●											
Coral				●												
TWO-TONE																
Sea-Mist Green / Neptune Green	●	●					●	●			●	●	●	●	●	●
Skyline Blue / Glacier Blue	●	●					●	●					●	●	●	
Neptune Green / Shoreline Beige			●													
India Ivory / Skyline Blue	●	●	●				●	●		●			●	●	●	
India Ivory / Shadow Gray	●	●				●							●	●	●	
Autumn Bronze / Shoreline Beige											●	●				
India Ivory / Sea-Mist Green							●	●		●						
Shoreline Beige / Autumn Bronze	●	●		●	●	●	●	●								●
Glacier Blue / Shoreline Beige							●	●		●						
India Ivory / Onyx Black										●						
India Ivory / Gypsy Red						●				●						
Glacier Blue / Skyline Blue				●							●	●				
India Ivory / Regal Turquoise	●	●	●	●		●										
Shoreline Beige / Neptune Green	●	●	●				●	●					●	●	●	
Shoreline Beige / Glacier Blue			●		●	●					●	●				
Shoreline Beige / Gypsy Red			●	●	●	●										
Onyx Black / India Ivory										●						
Shadow Gray / Coral	●	●	●			●										
Neptune Green / Sea-Mist Green				●	●	●										
India Ivory / Coral				●												
India Ivory / Harvest Gold	●	●	●	●		●				●						
India Ivory / Navajo Tan						●										
Regal Turquoise / India Ivory						●										

development of a brand-new chassis and drivetrain, again with weight-saving always in mind. What emerged was conventional but modern—and quite a departure for Chevrolet. Though wheelbase remained at 115 inches, the '55 frame was 18-percent lighter and 50-percent stiffer than the previous Chevy chassis, according to Cole, with less unsprung weight and more widely spaced siderails for better stability. "We got away from the heavy torque-tube drive and went to [open] Hotchkiss drive," he said. "We went to a Salisbury-type [rear] axle instead of the banjo type . . . ball-joint front suspension [and] tubular frame." The last actually referred to box-girder siderails. Convertibles got a central X-member for the extra stiffness that body style requires.

Trumpeted as "Glide-Ride," the new front suspension was described as a "spherical-joint design" (to avoid using Ford's "ball-joint" term) with "bearing surfaces of a new plastic material which is exceptionally long-wearing." Geometry comprised classic, unequal-length upper-and-lower A-arms acting on coil springs wound around life-sealed, double-acting hydraulic shock absorbers. Out back was the familiar live axle on parallel, longitudinal semi-elliptic leaf springs, but the springs were nine-inches longer (58 inches), wider (two inches), and newly mounted outboard of the main frame rails, thus dictating diagonal shock placement. Lube-free rear "spring leaf-end liners of impregnated webbing" were also featured. With the wider chassis and 6.70 x 15 four-ply tires (now tubeless as standard, as was the case nearly industry-wide), track measured 58 inches front, 58.8 inches rear.

Other mechanical highlights included switching from a six- to 12-volt electrical system (one year ahead of Ford) and adoption of recirculating-ball-and-nut steering with a 20:1 ratio. The self-energizing, 11-inch-diameter "Jumbo Drum" brakes returned with new lube-free nylon bushings.

Because Chevy was GM's biggest seller, styling for the all-new '55 was carefully considered. Pierre Ollier, a former body

Solid Colors for the 1955 Chevrolet

Harvest Gold	Onyx Black	Sea-Mist Green	Neptune Green	Skyline Blue	Glacier Blue	Copper Maroon
Shoreline Beige	Autumn Bronze	India Ivory	Shadow Gray	Gypsy Red	Regal Turquoise	Coral

Two-Tone Combinations

Sea-Mist Green / Neptune Green	Skyline Blue / Glacier Blue	Neptune Green / Shoreline Beige	India Ivory / Skyline Blue	India Ivory / Shadow Gray	Autumn Bronze / Shoreline Beige	India Ivory / Sea-Mist Green	Shoreline Beige / Autumn Bronze
Glacier Blue / Shoreline Beige	India Ivory / Onyx Black	India Ivory / Gypsy Red	Glacier Blue / Skyline Blue	India Ivory / Regal Turquoise	Shoreline Beige / Neptune Green	Shoreline Beige / Glacier Blue	Shoreline Beige / Gypsy Red
Onyx Black / India Ivory	Shadow Gray / Coral	Neptune Green / Sea-Mist Green	India Ivory / Coral	India Ivory / Harvest Gold	India Ivory / Navajo Tan	Regal Turquoise / India Ivory	

Buyers apparently liked the looks of the new '55 Chevy convertible (*opposite, top and this page*)—output more than doubled from 19,383 units in 1954 to 41,292 for '55. The mid-range Two-Ten Delray coupe (*opposite, bottom left*) retailed for $1835. (Owner: Fred Bender) The least expensive Bel Air, the two-door sedan (*opposite, bottom right*), cost $1888. (Owner: Charlie Baitinger)

designer in the company's commercial vehicle studios, recalled that serious design work got underway at about the same time as engineering, "around June 1952, at the GM Styling Building on Milwaukee Avenue in Detroit. Advance Body Design had begun with thousands of preliminary sketches . . . boiled them down to [a] handful, then rendered these in full-scale side view. But the final designs just wouldn't come, and [company styling chief] Harley Earl was getting increasingly upset. . . . [Early front-end themes] were slightly reminiscent of the [1952-53] Aero Willys, and proposed taillight designs were reaching a hopeless stage of tortured, overworked features. Suddenly, Earl blew his top, and that did wonders."

The result was largely the work of Chevy studio head Clare MacKichan, staff designer Carl H. Renner, and body engineer Charles A. Stebbins. Following Earl's dictum of "go all the way, then back off," they produced a knockout package only a bit less radical than initially envisioned. Uncommonly clean for the period, it was boxy, yet altogether sleeker and crisper than the stodgy 1953-54 models despite the unchanged wheelbase.

"Longer-Lower-Wider" was Detroit's order of the day, so overall height was slashed by up to six inches on wagons and 2.5 inches on other models, aided by the new chassis' lower ride height. Oddly, the '55 was about an inch shorter and narrower overall, but it *looked* longer and wider, thanks to Chevy's first fully flush rear fenders and a hood almost level with the front fenders.

Only one element proved controversial: the Ferrari-like, eggcrate rectangular grille. Earl liked its simplicity, but management didn't, favoring a shinier, full-width treatment that was also in the running (and adopted for '56). Some dealers didn't like it either, finding it a tough sell against the glittering dentistry of the '55 Ford and Plymouth. But as Renner observed: "Mr. Earl possessed much power. . . . And although some individuals did not agree with his decisions, being boss, he had his own way."

The '55 Chevy was unquestionably a Harley Earl design, and successfully combined a number of his favorite ideas. For example, the fashionable "Sweep Sight" wraparound windshield, also new to Chevy, dated from his 1951 LeSabre show car, the first Corvette, and the limited-edition 1953 Cadillac Eldorado and Oldsmobile Fiesta convertibles. The latter also introduced the rakish beltline dip or

From the exterior, the Two-Ten Delray and the Two-Ten two-door sedan were identical. The difference was inside, where the Delray sported a fancier vinyl interior to justify its $60-dollar higher price. Listing at $1775, the two-door sedan (*opposite page*) attracted 249,105 customers. This car's second color is on the roof only, although it could have been ordered with the white on the rear flanks and decklid as well. The chrome sidespear on the rear fenders of the Two-Ten was different than that of the Bel Air: a bit thinner and sans the white painted insert. Further, Bel Airs received nameplates and a Chevy crest above the sidespear, just behind the chrome slash. Note also the Two-Ten's plainer dashboard (*right*). (Owner: Jim Geraghty)

notch used on all models save wagons. MacKichan explained that this stemmed from Earl's fondness for low roofs. "He liked low windows [and] low rear quarters, so to get that feeling he wanted to raise the rear fender, and sometimes it was higher than the beltline. . . . That is how we got into that kind of dipped shape." Stylists also experimented with a hood set *lower* than the tops of the front fenders, then dismissed it as ungainly. Wagons featured curved rear side glass, an innovation for this increasingly popular body type that

answered growing buyer demand for less utilitarian looks.

Renner credits some of Earl's aesthetic preferences to his physical stature: "He was six-foot four, and mockups looked quite different to him than they would to an average-size person. Therefore . . . designers [sometimes] strapped blocks of wood to their shoes, which afforded them the same vantage point—all unknown to Mr. Earl, of course."

Two-toning helped sell cars in the mid-Fifties, and the new Chevy had some of

the best. It was most daring on non-wagon Bel Airs and Two-Tens. Roof, rear deck, and upper rear fenders wore one shade, with the bodyside color break defined by a horizontal chrome strip running rearward from a short "slash" molding at the beltline dip. The bottom-line One-Tens did without the side trim, so their contrasting colors were confined to the roof; this treatment could also be ordered on Bel Airs and Two-Tens. Hooded headlamps were also *de rigueur*, and these were nicely blended into the new flat-top front fenders. Chuck

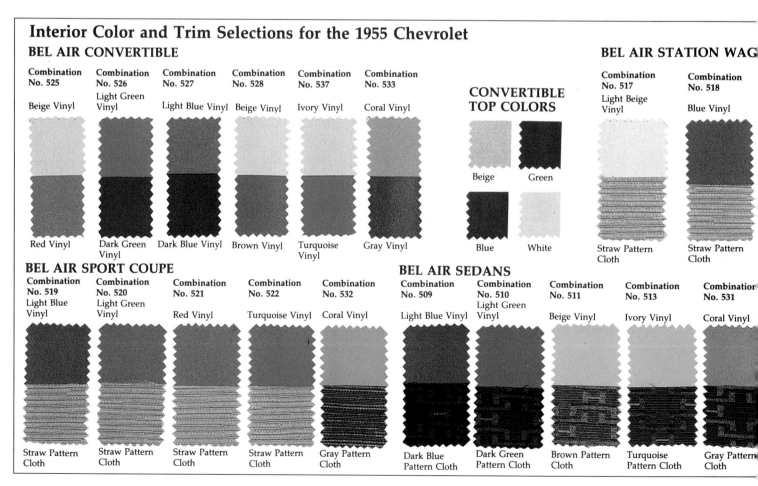

Interior Color and Trim Selections for the 1955 Chevrolet

BEL AIR CONVERTIBLE

Combination No. 525	Combination No. 526	Combination No. 527	Combination No. 528	Combination No. 537	Combination No. 533
Beige Vinyl	Light Green Vinyl	Light Blue Vinyl	Beige Vinyl	Ivory Vinyl	Coral Vinyl
Red Vinyl	Dark Green Vinyl	Dark Blue Vinyl	Brown Vinyl	Turquoise Vinyl	Gray Vinyl

CONVERTIBLE TOP COLORS

Beige	Green
Blue	White

BEL AIR STATION WAG[ON]

Combination No. 517	Combination No. 518
Light Beige Vinyl	Blue Vinyl
Straw Pattern Cloth	Straw Pattern Cloth

BEL AIR SPORT COUPE

Combination No. 519	Combination No. 520	Combination No. 521	Combination No. 522	Combination No. 532
Light Blue Vinyl	Light Green Vinyl	Red Vinyl	Turquoise Vinyl	Coral Vinyl
Straw Pattern Cloth	Straw Pattern Cloth	Straw Pattern Cloth	Straw Pattern Cloth	Gray Pattern Cloth

BEL AIR SEDANS

Combination No. 509	Combination No. 510	Combination No. 511	Combination No. 513	Combination No. 531
Light Blue Vinyl	Light Green Vinyl	Beige Vinyl	Ivory Vinyl	Coral Vinyl
Dark Blue Pattern Cloth	Dark Green Pattern Cloth	Brown Pattern Cloth	Turquoise Pattern Cloth	Gray Pattern [Cloth]

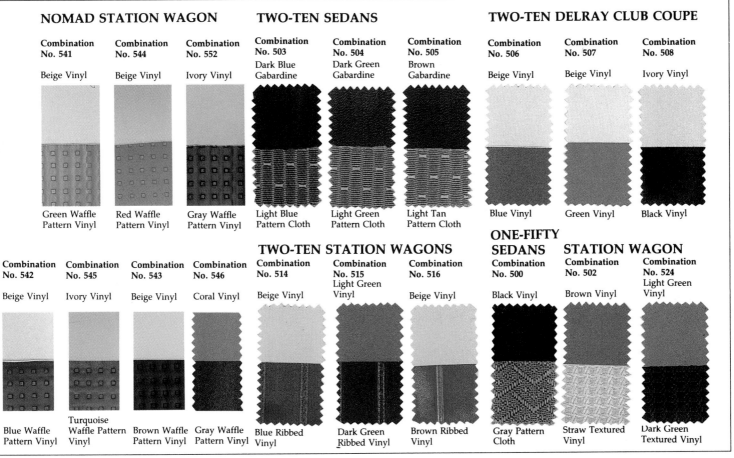

NOMAD STATION WAGON

Combination No. 541
Beige Vinyl
Green Waffle Pattern Vinyl

Combination No. 544
Beige Vinyl
Red Waffle Pattern Vinyl

Combination No. 552
Ivory Vinyl
Gray Waffle Pattern Vinyl

Combination No. 542
Beige Vinyl
Blue Waffle Pattern Vinyl

Combination No. 545
Ivory Vinyl
Turquoise Waffle Pattern Vinyl

Combination No. 543
Beige Vinyl
Brown Waffle Pattern Vinyl

Combination No. 546
Coral Vinyl
Gray Waffle Pattern Vinyl

TWO-TEN SEDANS

Combination No. 503
Dark Blue Gabardine
Light Blue Pattern Cloth

Combination No. 504
Dark Green Gabardine
Light Green Pattern Cloth

Combination No. 505
Brown Gabardine
Light Tan Pattern Cloth

TWO-TEN STATION WAGONS

Combination No. 514
Beige Vinyl
Blue Ribbed Vinyl

Combination No. 515
Light Green Vinyl
Dark Green Ribbed Vinyl

Combination No. 516
Beige Vinyl
Brown Ribbed Vinyl

TWO-TEN DELRAY CLUB COUPE

Combination No. 506
Beige Vinyl
Blue Vinyl

Combination No. 507
Beige Vinyl
Green Vinyl

Combination No. 508
Ivory Vinyl
Black Vinyl

ONE-FIFTY SEDANS

Combination No. 500
Black Vinyl
Gray Pattern Cloth

STATION WAGON

Combination No. 502
Brown Vinyl
Straw Textured Vinyl

Combination No. 524
Light Green Vinyl
Dark Green Textured Vinyl

Stebbins conceived the functional tail-lamps, which jutted out slightly from the rear fenders and could thus be seen from the sides, a useful safety feature. This design was originally intended to define a prominent horizontal decklid crease just above the license plate, with the sheetmetal below set back slightly for a sculptured effect. Here, Earl and Cole were overruled—apparently for cost reasons—by Harlow Curtice, named GM president in 1953 when "Engine Charlie" Wilson left to become Secretary of Defense in the Eisenhower Administration.

"Nothing was carried over," MacKichan said later. "With the new V-8 and the young man's image . . . we tried to get it more youthful. [Yet] there *was* a Cadillac feeling. . . . Those headlight eyebrows, the eagle hood ornament [a Carl Renner contribution], the wraparound windshield. And the taillights were designed to give a Cadillac look. . . . I don't think 'copy' is the right word, but the flavor [was] definitely there."

Interior alterations were just as extensive. Soft trim, developed by Ed Donaldson, was plusher and more expensive-looking than before, especially the Bel Air Nomad's new "waffle" patterned vinyl, while Renner's symmetrically arranged instrument panel

was refreshingly subdued next to Chevy's recent "jukebox" dashboards. Instruments nestled directly ahead of the wheel in a simple fan-shaped cluster that was matched on the right by the radio speaker housing, this "twin-cowl" motif had been introduced with the first Corvette. Bel Air panels wore a full-width *appliqué* embossed with tiny versions of the Chevy "bowtie" logo—987 of them for those who cared to count. Enhancing comfort was a new "High Level" ventilation system, via a mesh-covered air

intake on the topside of the cowl.

Introduced under the "Motoramic" label, Chevrolet's 1955 lineup initially comprised 14 models in the same three series as 1953-54. A Two-Ten Sport Coupe hardtop arrived in June 1955, while that most singular of wagons, the two-door Nomad, joined the top-line Bel Air group in February.

The Nomad is a story in itself. Significant as the first production car to combine the best design attributes of station wagon

A new mid-year '55 model from Chevy was the Two-Ten two-door hardtop (*opposite, bottom*). At $1959 ($2058 with V-8), it undercut the Bel Air Sport Coupe by $108. Most buyers, however, felt that the more deluxe Bel Air trim was worth the extra money. Thus, only 11,675 Two-Ten hardtops were built for '55, compared to 185,562 Bel Airs. This car has the standard small hubcaps, but sports the optional grille guard, fuel filler guard, and two-tone paint. Most two-toned Two-Tens and Bel Airs placed the lighter color (often India Ivory) at the rear and on the roof. But not always, as this two-tone blue Bel Air ragtop shows (*opposite, top and this page*)—the darker shade is up back. And with its white top, it's actually a three-tone car. (Owner: Paul Eggerling)

and hardtop coupe—the Fifties' two most influential body styles—it was another Harley Earl idea, though MacKichan's staff first suggested a "sport wagon" as one of two additions to the '55 line. (The other, a long-deck, three-window "Executive Coupe," never got off the drawing board.) "The Corvette theme was a popular one," MacKichan recalled, and "Carl Renner . . . had come up with a sketch for a station wagon roof that caught Earl's eye. Bringing this idea to the Chevrolet studio, Earl asked

that it be incorporated into a station wagon version as one of [three] Corvette idea cars for the 1954 Motorama."

Thus was born the Corvette Nomad, a non-running exercise with fiberglass bodywork on a conventional 1953 Chevrolet station wagon chassis. Renner's roof nicely suited the lower body lines of Chevy's recently announced sports car, and the stylists couldn't have picked a better name. First seen in January 1954 at New York's Waldorf-Astoria Hotel, the Corvette

Nomad was such a hit that Earl's assistant, Howard O'Leary, hurriedly called MacKichan and ordered its roof styling adapted for the new standard Chevrolet—giving him just two days to do it.

Renner hustled. "The [show car's] roof was taken from a full-size drawing, cut apart, stretched out, and mated to the . . . 1955 Chevrolet lower body," said MacKichan. "The hardtop front-door glass framing, forward-sloping rear quarters, wide B-pillar, fluted roof, wraparound rear side glass, the rear wheel housing cutout, and the seven vertical accent strips on the tailgate [later nicknamed "bananas" by enthusiasts] were all retained in a remarkably good translation from the dream car." Aside from all-steel bodywork, the production Bel Air Nomad differed in using a conventional liftgate—a heavy, chrome-plated die-cast affair—instead of the show

This page: What became the '55 Chevy Bel Air Nomad began as the Corvette Nomad show car (*top*), which was shown at the '54 GM Motorama. Deemed too expensive for the limited-output 'Vette, the design was transferred to the '55 Chevy, seen here on November 3, 1954 (*center and bottom*). *Opposite page*: The '55 Nomad bowed with a pricey $2571 price tag. (Owner: Bob Flack)

car's drop-down tailgate window. The "fluted roof" refers to nine transverse grooves at the rear, a visual remnant of Earl's plan for a telescoping stainless-steel section that was quickly precluded by leak worries and projected high cost.

Pontiac got a Nomad too, the Safari, but only at the last minute and—predictably— over Chevrolet's objections. Alas, the marriage of hardtop flair and wagon utility wasn't bliss in either version. Though it looked like other '55 Chevys, the Nomad shared little with them aft of the cowl and was thus the most expensive Chevy ever: $2571 with V-8—$265 more than a similarly equipped Bel Air convertible and $210 more than the four-door Bel Air Beauville wagon, which the ever-quotable "Uncle" Tom McCahill of *Mechanix Illustrated* jested was "large enough to carry a troop of polar bears, [250-pound friend] Jim McMichael and a scale model of Mount Vesuvius." Surely the lack of four doors limited the Nomad's appeal, especially among wagon buyers. Then too, the glassy interior was great for visibility but uncomfortably warm on sunny days, the liftgate sucked in exhaust fumes when open, and the slanted rear was prone to water leaks. With all this, the Nomad was Chevy's least popular '55, garnering only 8386 orders, just one-third as many as the Beauville. Of course, it's long been the most collectible for that very reason, as well as its handsome looks—and the fact that it's a '55 Chevy.

The 1955 Chevy was greeted with near universal acclaim. Veteran tester Tom McCahill called it "a junior-size Olds with Buick doors and a Cadillac rear, the most glamorous-looking and hottest-performing Chevy to come down the pike... [and] rugged competition for Ford in the scramble to see which American car will outsell all others."

While performance was expected from the new V-8, fine roadability was a pleasant surprise. "Best-handling Chevrolet I have ever driven," reported Floyd Clymer in *Popular Mechanics*, "and it feels like a large car." *Motor Trend*'s editors named Chevy (along with the '55 Mercury) the year's top handler. Said Walt Woron: "That mushy feeling, so long associated with the American automobile, is gone. In its place is . . . solid sureness, a willingness to be steered, not aimed [and his car didn't have power assist]. . . . When we deliberately drove it off the shoulder, [it] wouldn't whip so as to cause us to lose control. . . . We could throw it into turns at practically any speed, [even those] that would make other

cars quail." Even the usually dour *Consumer Reports* saw fit to give the '55 Chevy special mention for handling in its price class.

Criticisms were surprisingly few for a mass-production car. Ride was generally judged a bit hard, while *Road & Track* magazine found the steering woefully slow at 4.5 turns lock-to-lock, and felt handling had "plenty of room for improvement." Some testers, such as Floyd Clymer of *Popular Mechanics*, deplored the switch from gauges to warning lights for oil pressure and generator; he commented that "I prefer gauges that tell what is happening as well as what is not." Others found seat travel insufficient and the steering wheel too high and close. *Consumer Reports*, meanwhile, observed some swerve in braking on all three of its test cars.

But such quibbles were easily overshadowed by styling that most everybody liked and V-8 go that had everybody talking. The "old man's" car was dead:

This well-optioned '55 Bel Air Sport Coupe (*both pages*) is equipped with most of the available chrome goodies: grille guard, front and rear fender guards, rocker panel trim, and more. It also sports fender skirts. (Owner: Richard Kalinowski) A Chevy styling study dated January 27, 1955 (*top right and above*), featured a revised greenhouse. Note the rear wheel opening.

long live "The Hot One!" Even in basic, 162-bhp form, the 265 was both stronger and thriftier than Plymouth's new 260-cid V-8 or Ford's enlarged 272 Y-block—and it had a bit less weight to haul.

The figures told the story. Clymer's Powerglide-equipped Bel Air topped 108 mph, while *Motor Trend*'s 180-bhp car did 0-60 mph in 11.4 seconds (in Low range), the standing quarter-mile in 18.4 seconds, and the 50-80-mph spurt (with Low held to 60 mph) in 12.9 seconds. *Road & Track* got the best numbers by ordering the stick-overdrive/Power-Pack combo in a light Two-Ten two-door: 9.7 seconds 0-60 mph, 17.2 seconds in the standing quarter-mile. Fuel economy? A creditable 18-22 miles per gallon.

Such formidable performance inevitably led to competition, beginning with the Daytona Speed Weeks in February. Jack Radtke finished 10th overall in the traditional road-and-beach race against Buicks,

Not only does this '55 Bel Air soft-top (*left*) sport all of the extra-cost exterior goodies, it also boasts a continental rear tire, giving it an impression of added length. Note the traffic light viewer on the dash. (Owner: Chuck Sarges) One of the brightest color choices for the ragtop was India Ivory over Harvest Gold (*above*). (Owner: Bill Ferguson)

Oldsmobiles, and Chrysler 300s, while other Chevys took the top four spots in class and eight of the first 11 positions. In the two-way measured mile, three more Chevys were among the five fastest cars with engines of 250-299 cid. Soon, "Smokey" Yunick entered a V-8 Chevy in

National Association for Stock Car Automobile Racing (NASCAR) short-track contests, where it proved unbeatable in the hands of former Hudson Hornet pilot Herb Thomas. It was equally capable in NASCAR's longer Grand National events, with Thomas and Fonty Flock often

The '55 Bel Air Sport Coupe, seen here in India Ivory over Onyx Black (*both pages*), rode a 115-inch wheelbase and weighed in at a relatively modest 3180 pounds. That compared with a 115.5-inch chassis for the '55 Ford Victoria hardtop, which came in at 3251 pounds. Plymouth, meanwhile, had an identical 115-inch wheel span, but weighed 3261 pounds in Belvedere Sport Coupe form. Overall, the Ford was about three inches longer than the Chevy, Plymouth (at 203.8 inches) eight inches longer. Though competition was keen, the Chevy hardtop outsold both of its competitors. The Bel Air Sport Coupe's interior (*opposite*) featured a combination of "Straw Pattern" cloth and vinyl. Compare this with the all-vinyl convertible interiors seen on earlier pages. (Owner: Michael Polsinelli)

winning against much larger and more powerful machinery.

Observing these early exploits, Ed Cole began issuing certain heavy-duty "export" parts through dealers, a ploy other makes were using to get their best hardware into racers' hands. It paid off. Thomas won the Southern 500 at Darlington, South Carolina, on Labor Day at an average 92.281 mph, followed by Jim Reed in another Chevy. Tim Flock, Fonty's brother, was third in a Chrysler 300, but Chevys also finished fourth, seventh, and eighth through 10th—*seven* of the first 10 finishers. October brought a repeat performance at Charlotte, and Chevy ran 1-2 at Atlanta. Meanwhile, another ex-Hudson driver, Marshall Teague, began dominating the American Automobile Association circuit. Symbolizing Chevy's new performance prowess, a Bel Air convertible was selected as the Official Pace Car for this year's Indy 500. In all, 1955 was the greatest competition year for a low-price make in years.

It was certainly a great year for Chevy buyers, who could now personalize their cars more than ever. Air conditioning, a compact unit that took up no trunk space, was the most expensive extra at $565—and thus not often ordered—but others were downright cheap. The base V-8, for example, cost a mere $99, overdrive added $108, power steering $92, and "Pivot Pedal" power brakes just $38. Also available were a $123 "Wheel Carrier Continental" tire, manual-tune and Custom signal-seeking radios, recirculating heater/defroster, DeLuxe heater, windshield washer, electric clock, parking brake warning lamp, full wheel covers (standard on the Bel Air), and all the usual chrome exterior embellishments: grille guard, body sill moldings, exhaust extensions, side window ventshades, and shields for fenders, door handles, and gas filler flap. Interior extras included floormats, accelerator pedal cover, chrome-plated tissue dispenser, compass, a "Glamour Glide" front seat cushion protector of "rich nylon-dacron," luggage compartment lamp, portable underhood spotlight, and a "four-contour" GM electric shaver "for use in car or home."

But the most interesting item in Chevy's 1955 color, trim, and accessories book is the one that didn't actually appear for another three years—and then only on a Cadillac. This was the "Automatic Top Raiser," a typically Fifties gadget that Harley Earl had been toying with on various show cars for some time. Described as "a new, modern electronic device that will automatically raise a convertible's top at the first drops of rain when the car is unattended," it was subsequently withdrawn, no doubt due to technical problems. The only time it saw "production" was when Cadillac used it on five mildly modified 1958 Eldorado Biarritz convertibles built for that year's auto show season.

In retrospect, the 1955 Chevrolet was a stunning achievement that marked a turning point for "USA-1." Seldom had a mass-market Detroiter been so completely transformed in one year—or so successfully. All of a sudden, a name once synonymous with dull-but-durable low-price transportation had a bright new luster of youthful zest, sizzling performance, and race-proved stamina. And despite stronger-than-ever competition, Chevy solidified its position as industry sales leader, beating Ford by some 230,000 units in model year production and by nearly 66,000 for the calendar year.

As might perhaps be expected, the mid-line Two-Ten series was Chevy's best seller

in 1955 with 805,309 units built in all body styles. The upmarket Bel Air wasn't far behind, however, as 773,238 were produced. The low-bucks One-Fifty trailed way behind as only 134,257 found buyers, and many of those ended up being fleet cars—Americans were clearly demanding, and willing to pay for, cars with more amenities and style, even in the low-price field. The grand total of 1,704,667 cars was a Chevy production record that must have been cause for the popping of champagne corks on the 14th floor of the General Motors Building on Grand Avenue in Detroit.

Only one question now remained: What would Chevy do for an encore?

Times were good in 1955, particularly for General Motors, which had over the years cornered an ever-larger share of the U.S. automobile market. It was now commanding about half of it, and that year brought even more cause for celebration as noted in a press release (when GM later produced its 100 millionth car): "On November 23, 1954, the 50 millionth automobile produced by General Motors in the United States rolled off a Chevrolet assembly line in Flint, Michigan, to be welcomed by GM officials, civic leaders, newsmen and photographers. In addition to a fitting ceremony at the plant, civic luncheons were held in 65 cities from coast to coast and General Motors plants across the country held Open House to more than a million people." The car taking the honors was a gold '55 Bel Air Sport Coupe (*both pages*). *Opposite page, bottom*: A sampling of '55 Chevy accessories.

1955

Accessories

Fender antenna
Self deicing wiper blade
Wiring junction block
Power brakes
Locking gas cap
Continental wheel carrier
Electric clock
Compass
Nylon/plastic/fiber seat covers
Accelerator pedal cover
Wheel covers
Wire wheel covers
Tissue dispenser
Exhaust extension
Oil filter and element
License plate frame
Glareshades
Grille guard
Fender guard
Door edge guard
Gasoline filler guard
Heater and defroster
Tool kit
Back-up lamps
Courtesy lamps
Cigarette lighter
Floor mats

Outside rearview mirrors
Inside non-glare rearview mirror
Vanity visor
Body sill molding
Radio: manual, push-button, or
    signal-seeking
Automatic top raiser (convertible)
Arm rests
Wheel trim rings
Safetylight with mirror
Power-positioned front seat
Electric shaver
Parking brake signal
Door handle shields
Front fender shields
Rear seat speaker
Spotlamp
Power steering
Whitewall tires
Ventshades
Outside visors
Inside visors
Traffic light viewer
Windshield washer (vacuum or
    foot-operated)
Electric-power window lifts

1955 Chevrolet Specifications, Prices, and Production

Model	Overall Length	Curb Weight	List Price	Production
1955 (115-inch wheelbase)				
ONE-FIFTY				
1502 Sedan, two-door	195.6	3,145	1,685	99,146
1503 Sedan, four-door	195.6	3,150	1,728	29,898
1512 Sedan, utility	195.6	3,070	1,593	11,196
1529 Handyman, two-door wagon	197.1	3,275	2,030	17,936
TWO-TEN				
2102 Sedan, two-door	195.6	3,130	1,775	249,105
2103 Sedan, four-door	195.6	3,165	1,819	317,724
2109 Townsman, four-door wagon	197.1	3,335	2,127	82,303
2124 Delray, coupe	195.6	3,130	1,835	115,584
2129 Handyman, two-door wagon	197.1	3,315	2,079	28,918
2154 Hardtop, coupe	195.6	3,155	1,959	11,675
BEL AIR				
2402 Sedan, two-door	195.6	3,140	1,888	168,313
2403 Sedan, four-door	195.6	3,185	1,932	345,372
2409 Beauville, four-door wagon	197.1	3,370	2,262	24,313
2429 Nomad, two-door wagon	197.1	3,285	2,472	8,386
2434 Convertible, coupe	195.6	3,300	2,206	41,292
2454 Sport Coupe, hardtop	195.6	3,180	2,067	185,562

Engine/Transmission Availability

	cid	bore/stroke (inches)	compression ratio	bhp @ rpm	carb	trans
1955						
Six	235	3.56 × 3.94	7.5:1	123 @ 3800	1V	3-sp., OD
Six	235	3.56 × 3.94	7.5:1	136 @ 4200	1V	PG[1]
V-8	265	3.75 × 3.00	8.0:1	162 @ 4400	2V	3-sp., OD, PG[1]
V-8	265	3.75 × 3.00	8.0:1	180 @ 4600	4V	3-sp., OD, PG[1]

[1]Powerglide

1956

"THE HOT ONE'S EVEN HOTTER!"

After a rousing 1955, fans might have wondered what Chevrolet would do for 1956. They needn't have worried, for there would be more style (bigger and more "important" looking), more power, and more refinements—all geared "to make the going sweeter."

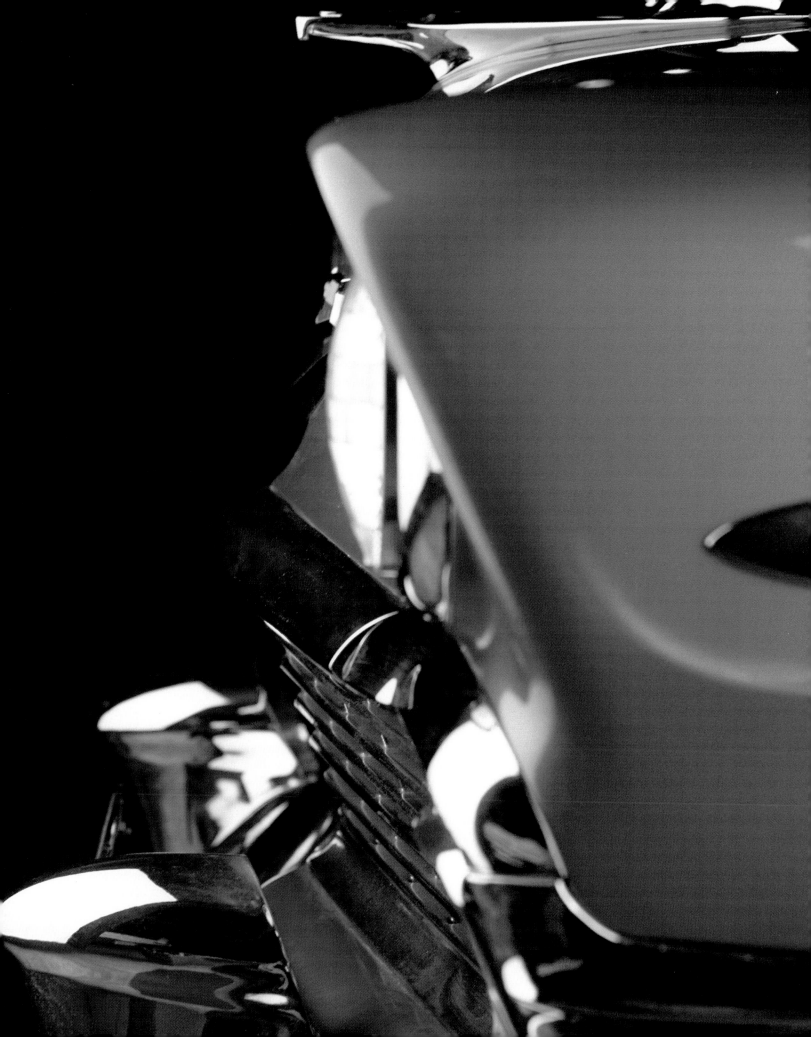

Given the revolutionary changes that Chevrolet had undergone for 1955, one could reasonably wonder what Chevy would do for a follow up in 1956. Anyone familiar with the more-or-less traditional three-year styling cycle in Detroit, however, knew without a doubt that the '56 would be a facelifted version of the '55. But what surprised many people at the time was the extent of both the facelift and the engineering upgrades. That may have seemed impressive in 1956, but to latterday observers who can compare the 1955, '56, *and* '57 models simultaneously, the '56 ends up too often being thought of as a "middle child."

Middle children, as is well known, tend to be slighted in many families, and the 1956 Chevrolet is no exception. Though revered as a "classic" Chevy, it's long been eclipsed in enthusiast affections by the trailblazing '55 and the speedier, shinier '57. That's unfortunate. In many ways, the '56 was the best of both worlds: faster and flashier than its predecessor, yet closer than its successor to the lithe simplicity of Ed Cole's original concept.

It was certainly the most successful "classic" Chevy in commercial terms, a fact that has been largely ignored. Despite a broad sales retreat industry-wide, not unexpected after record-breaking 1955, Detroit nonetheless built nearly 6.3 million cars for model year '56. Chevrolet claimed no less than 44.4 percent of Big Three low-price sales as its total market share rose from 24 percent, which was actually down about two points on 1954, to 27.9 percent—the highest of the three "classic" years. Remarkably, Chevy managed this on just 88 percent of its 1955 volume. By contrast, Ford fell to 77 percent of its previous output and Plymouth plunged to 60 percent. Plymouth's slide helped Dearborn grab a 23.7-percent slice of the industry pie, up 1.5 percent from '55.

The car that worked these wonders for America's favorite make could easily be dismissed as a warmed-up '55—which it mostly *was*—though that was hardly bad considering what Chevrolet had to warm up. Besides, conventional design wisdom in mid-Fifties Detroit was that to sell well, a car had to *look* new even if it wasn't— particularly if it was a ground-up-fresh design from the year before. Industry critics called this "planned obsolescence."

Mastering that art well before anyone else had been a major factor in helping General Motors achieve industry dominance by the early Fifties. So there was no question that the '56 Chevrolet would be

This page: Planning for the '56 Chevrolet began well before the '55 debuted, but it was known that 1956 would be a facelift year and that the doors, rear deck, and roof would have to be carried over. By May 3, 1954, the taillamp design seemed well in hand (*top*), though side trim options were undecided. An August 9, 1954 proposal (*above*) strutted a bolder '55-style grille, and side trim that was ultimately adopted for the '56 One-Fifty series. Exhausts exiting through the rear bumper were considered in January 1955 (*right*), but dropped. *Opposite page*: Compare a May 21, 1954 clay (*top row*), as well as the two-door side of the same car (*second row from top*), with the August proposal on the opposite page. August 30 brought a four-door hardtop (*third row from top*), with Chevy taillights on one side, Pontiac units on the other. An October 1954 clay wears the '56 front end (*bottom left*), and by November the Bel Air side trim was pretty much in place (*bottom right*).

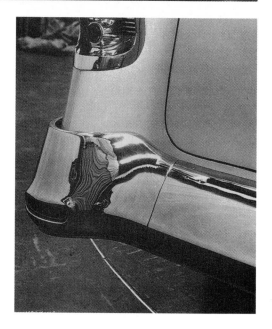

A Chevy Bel Air Sport Sedan four-door hardtop (*top*) is shown parked next to a group of large "chips" of 1956 color offerings. This car is painted in India Ivory and Dusk Plum. Another car in this new-for-1956 Sport Sedan body style is shown in Onyx Black and Crocus Yellow (*bottom*). The base price came in at $2320. The two-door Sport Coupe (*center*) retailed at $2176 for 1956, $144 less than the four-door—but $109 more than the '55 Sport Coupe.

as visually different from the '55 as possible, albeit within the monetary bounds of Detroit's three-year life cycle of new design/minor facelift/major facelift. Still, the sums lavished on the '56 Chevy were extravagant even for that free-spending decade. The restyle alone cost no less than $40 million, with $1 million just for the front fenders!

Of course, there was a reason. Chevrolet had begun planning for the '56 well before the '55 had actually appeared in dealer showrooms, and some division managers were likely nervous about public reaction to such a radically different Chevy. They needn't have worried, as we know, but they didn't have the benefit of hindsight. All they knew in early 1954 was that they were locked into this basic design for three years, and if buyers didn't go for it in 1955, recovery would hinge on the changes made for '56.

This was the thinking that shaped the in-between "classic" Chevy as much as contemporary market trends, which increasingly favored bigger, brighter cars with more horsepower and better performance. The '56 complied on all counts.

According to Chevy design studio chief Clare MacKichan, the '56 styling brief called for a more "imposing" front end "and a little more chrome on the sides" than the '55. But by the time his staff had finished, they'd changed all sheetmetal below the beltline save the doors and decklid. The result was an even-more-Cadillac-like look than in 1955: bulkier, though not heavy-looking. In fact, it was one of the era's better facelifts, relatively conservative and astutely executed.

Specifically, the '55's small, understated grille gave way to a shiny full-width latticework incorporating a large, square parking lamp at each end. Above was a flatter, four-inch-longer hood bearing a large Chevy emblem, a wide chrome "V" on V-8 models, and a new stylized jet plane ornament. Front fenders were broader, headlamp eyebrows reshaped to suit, and a larger front bumper appeared with a slight central "vee," echoing hoodfront contour.

Along the flanks, wheel openings were

Chevy styling was fairly extensively revised for 1956 (*top*): new full-width grille, hood, front and rear fenders, and taillights. Ford (*center*) kept all of its 1955 sheetmetal, but updated the grille, taillights, and trim. Plymouth (*bottom*) fell in between: new rear fenders with modest tailfins, revised grille and side trim. All boasted more power. The models shown: Chevy Bel Air Sport Coupe (Owner: Sherry Echols), Ford Fairlane Crown Victoria (Owner: Howard C. Jezop), Plymouth Belvedere convertible (Owner: Jim Clark).

rounder and more rakishly flared, and L-shaped side trim dressed up the previously bare One-Fifty models, allowing them to be ordered with optional two-tone bodyside paint for the first time. This change forced Ford to add a bit of extra side trim to its base Mainline series later in the model year. Two-Tens and Bel Airs, meanwhile, wore more elaborate moldings that gave them bolder two-toning.

Bringing up the rear were extended fenders with large, chrome-plated clusters nestling in vertically cut notches. Each housed an (extra-cost) rectangular backup

The Bel Air Nomad (*above*) looked more like the regular Chevys for 1956. Though available for the full model year, sales slipped to 7886 units. Note the "bananas" on the tailgate. (Owner: Bruce Dockery) With output reaching 103,602 units, the new Bel Air Sport Sedan (*below*) was a rousing success. (Owner: Mr. Mahon)

lamp between a conical taillamp above (much as in 1953) and a small, round reflector in a bullet-shaped pod below. The left unit opened from the top to reveal a newly hidden fuel filler *a la* Cadillac. Though Chevrolet resisted the finny uplifts of this year's Plymouth and Dodge, its '56 tail sported the same general air in a more subtle way. A deeper-section back bumper provided the finishing touch.

Overall, the '56 was clearly busier than the '55—but it was more in tune with the times. Of course, GM design chief Harley Earl knew salable styling better than anyone. Was he now having second thoughts about the '55? "Very possibly," as MacKichan told *Collectible Automobile®* magazine. "Whatever ideas people had when the '56 was being done were carry-overs from when the '55 was done [and] Earl finally agreed that maybe the bigger grille would be alright for the '56. . . . I think his mind was changing at the time, though some of his earlier cars had quite a lot of chrome on the sides. Many times I

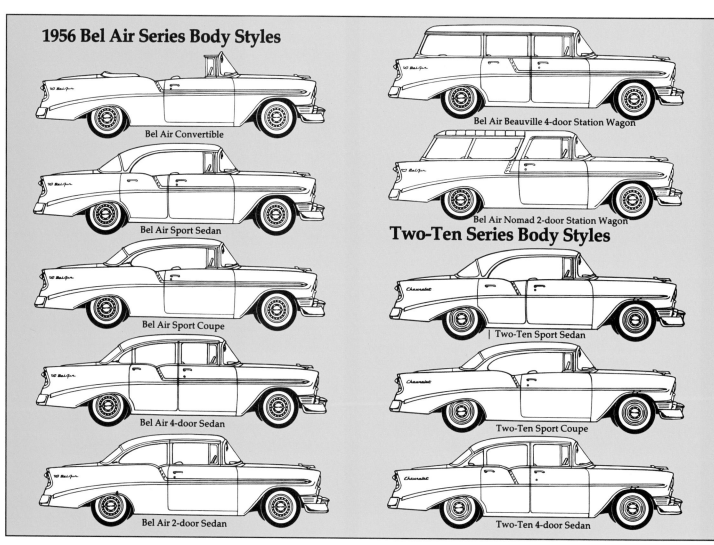

1956 Bel Air Series Body Styles

Bel Air Convertible

Bel Air Sport Sedan

Bel Air Sport Coupe

Bel Air 4-door Sedan

Bel Air 2-door Sedan

Bel Air Beauville 4-door Station Wagon

Bel Air Nomad 2-door Station Wagon

Two-Ten Series Body Styles

Two-Ten Sport Sedan

Two-Ten Sport Coupe

Two-Ten 4-door Sedan

The best seller among the '56 Bel Airs was the four-door sedan (*far left*)—it enjoyed better than a two-to-one margin over the second best seller, the Sport Coupe. In all, 269,798 Bel Air four-doors left the assembly lines during the model year. Base price was $2068, but about $100 extra bought a V-8, which was noted with a big "V" on the front of the hood (*left*). Bel Airs sported two-tone interior door trim (*above*). (Owner: Ronn Pittman)

heard him remark that you need 'entertainment' on the side of a car."

Though width, height, and wheelbase stayed virtually the same, the '56's fore and aft revisions added 2-3 inches in overall length for a total of 200.8 inches on wagons and 197.5 on other body styles. Together with the new side trim, they made appearance more streamlined. Interior dimensions and the basic '55 instrument panel weren't changed either, but there were the usual new colors and upholstery materials, and simple rectangular slots replaced the myriad of trademark "bowties" on the Bel Air dash appliqué.

Chevy's '56 lineup was as much in tune with the times as its styling. The three familiar series now spanned 19 models—three more than in 1955—plus 11 powerteams, 10 solid colors, and 14 two-tone combinations. Included was a new body style, the four-door hardtop, a GM first from 1955 (at Buick and Olds) that was adopted by most other makes this year. Called Sport Sedan and available in both

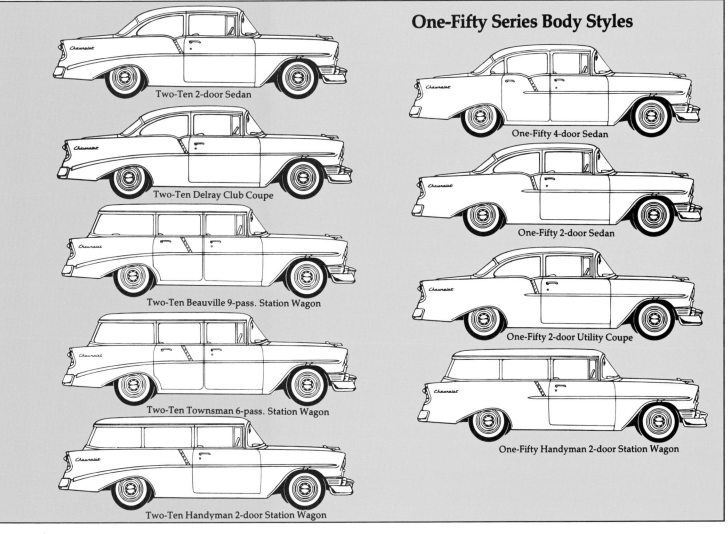

One-Fifty Series Body Styles

Two-Ten 2-door Sedan

Two-Ten Delray Club Coupe

Two-Ten Beauville 9-pass. Station Wagon

Two-Ten Townsman 6-pass. Station Wagon

Two-Ten Handyman 2-door Station Wagon

One-Fifty 4-door Sedan

One-Fifty 2-door Sedan

One-Fifty 2-door Utility Coupe

One-Fifty Handyman 2-door Station Wagon

Two-Ten and Bel Air versions, it was advertised as "embodying the youthful lines of a convertible, the practicality of a hardtop, and the convenience of a sedan." With wagon sales rising, Chevy switched the Bel Air Beauville from six- to nine-passenger seating and issued a Two-Ten counterpart, bringing wagon offerings to six. Other models were continued from '55.

The swanky Nomad wagon bowed with the rest of the line this time, and Chevy hoped that a full year's availability would push sales past the 10,000 mark. *Motor Trend* named it one of the year's most beautiful cars while admitting that "its distinct personal-car feel forces certain limiting features . . . [such as] the low roofline, compact overall package, sharply sloping rear." Yet former GM stylist Pierre Ollier disputes the myth that "Nomads traded off interior space for sporty looks.

. . . The Nomad had more cargo capacity with the second seat up than the 1955 Buick, Studebaker, Rambler, and several other contemporary wagons. With its rear seat [folded, it] had a longer cargo floor than 1955 Dodge, Ford, Plymouth, Rambler, and Stude wagons."

Nevertheless, Nomad still suffered from having just two doors instead of four, not to mention a high price. The latter prompted a bit of cost-cutting this year. Seat inserts

were borrowed from standard Bel Air hardtops and the Beauville, replacing the previous "waffle" material, and all exterior trim was now stock Bel Air save the sparkling tailgate "bananas" and, unique to the '56, a small chrome "V" below each taillamp (other Chevys signified a V-8 with one large "V" on decklid or tailgate). A nice detail touch was reversing the Bel Air's short rear-quarter "slash" moldings to match the angle of the slanted B-pillars.

Alas, base price rose more than $130, to $2608 with the base six-cylinder engine, and production over the full model year declined to 7886 units, just 0.50 percent of Chevy's total '56 volume. By comparison, the mid-year '55 had a much shorter selling season and accounted for 0.49 percent of model year sales.

Singular though the Nomad may have been, there was a far more unique and rarer '56 Chevy: the El Morroco. This one

Chevy built 128,382 Sport Coupe two-door hardtops for 1956, but *very* few of them came equipped with that year's ultimate engine: the 265 with dual four-barrel carburetors, the first of the famous "Duntov" cams, lightweight valves, and larger intake and exhaust passages. Horsepower came in at a rousing 225 at 5200 rpm. This particular example has the three-speed column-mounted manual shift, which only enhances the performance.

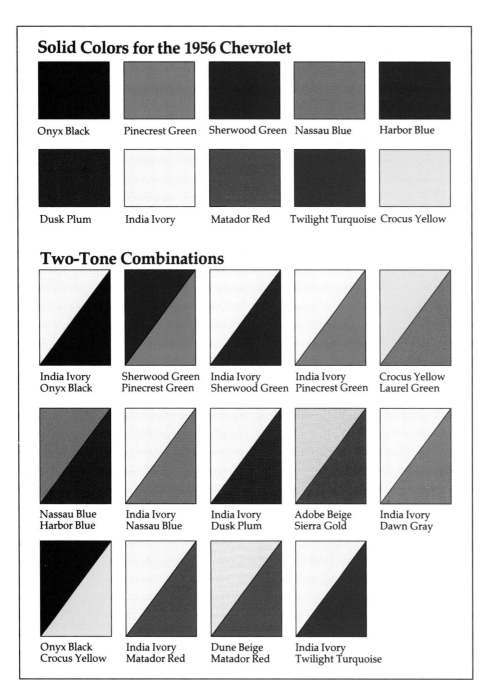

Solid Colors for the 1956 Chevrolet

Onyx Black | Pinecrest Green | Sherwood Green | Nassau Blue | Harbor Blue

Dusk Plum | India Ivory | Matador Red | Twilight Turquoise | Crocus Yellow

Two-Tone Combinations

India Ivory / Onyx Black | Sherwood Green / Pinecrest Green | India Ivory / Sherwood Green | India Ivory / Pinecrest Green | Crocus Yellow / Laurel Green

Nassau Blue / Harbor Blue | India Ivory / Nassau Blue | India Ivory / Dusk Plum | Adobe Beige / Sierra Gold | India Ivory / Dawn Gray

Onyx Black / Crocus Yellow | India Ivory / Matador Red | Dune Beige / Matador Red | India Ivory / Twilight Turquoise

1956 COLORS	Bel-Air		
	2-door Sedan	4-door Sedan	Sport Sedan
SOLID COLORS			
Onyx Black	●	●	●
Pinecrest Green	●	●	●
Sherwood Green	●	●	●
Nassau Blue	●	●	●
Harbor Blue	●	●	●
Dusk Plum	●	●	●
India Ivory	●	●	●
Matador Red	●	●	●
Twilight Turquoise	●	●	●
Crocus Yellow	●	●	●
TWO-TONE			
India Ivory / Onyx Black	●	●	●
Sherwood Green / Pinecrest Green	●	●	●
India Ivory / Sherwood Green	●	●	●
India Ivory / Pinecrest Green	●	●	●
Crocus Yellow / Laurel Green	●	●	●
Nassau Blue / Harbor Blue	●	●	●
India Ivory / Nassau Blue	●	●	●
India Ivory / Dusk Plum	●	●	●
Adobe Beige / Sierra Gold	●	●	●
India Ivory / Dawn Gray	●	●	●
Onyx Black / Crocus Yellow	●	●	●
India Ivory / Matador Red	●	●	
Dune Beige / Matador Red			●
India Ivory / Twilight Turquoise	●	●	●

Convertible Top Colors: I-Ivory; B-Blue; S-Black; T-Tan

wasn't built by Chevrolet, however, but by millionaire Detroit industrialist and car enthusiast Ruben Allender. Impressed by the Cadillac-inspired styling of the '56 Chevy, he reckoned in late 1955 that a market existed for a low-price look-alike of the Cadillac Eldorado convertible he'd just purchased—a car at the top of most everyone's "dream" list. Aware of the customizing craze then sweeping the nation, he decided to do what thousands were already doing: restyle a Chevrolet. The difference was that he would build copies to special order.

Besides having lots of money, he just happened to own a big warehouse on Van Dyke Avenue in Detroit, near Jefferson Avenue, filled with leftover hardware that could be used to create his automotive illusion. Allender went to Creative Industries, an independent Detroit specialty styling and fabrication house, which came up with a handsomely customized '56 Bel Air convertible that looked like a scaled-down Eldorado Biarritz. He then found a production engineer and shop manager, Cyril Olbrich, and made a deal with nearby Don McCoullagh Chevrolet to supply factory-fresh Bel Airs at about $50 over dealer cost.

Allender didn't stop there, however. Deciding that his cars should have their

Exterior Color Selections for the 1956 Chevrolet

Sport Coupe	Convertible	Beauville 9-pass. Wagon	Nomad	Two-Ten 2-door Sedan	Two-Ten 4-door Sedan	Two-Ten Sport Sedan	Two-Ten Sport Coupe	Two-Ten Delray Club Coupe	Two-Ten Beauville 9-pass. Wagon	Two-Ten Townsman 4-door Wagon	Two-Ten Handyman 2-door Wagon	One-Fifty 2-door Sedan	One-Fifty 4-door Sedan	One-Fifty Utility Sedan	One-Fifty Handyman 2-door Wagon
●	I,S	●	●	●	●	●	●	●	●	●	●	●	●	●	●
●	I,S,T	●		●	●	●	●	●	●	●	●	●	●	●	●
●	I,T			●	●	●	●	●	●	●	●	●	●	●	●
●	I,B,T	●		●	●	●	●	●	●	●	●	●	●	●	●
●	I,B,T			●	●	●	●								
●	I,T	●		●	●	●	●	●							
●	I,S	●		●	●	●	●	●	●	●	●	●	●	●	●
●	I,S	●		●	●	●	●	●	●	●	●	●	●	●	
●	I,S,T	●		●	●	●	●	●	●	●	●	●	●	●	
●	I,S	●		●	●	●	●	●	●	●	●	●	●	●	●
●	I,S	●	●	●	●	●	●	●	●	●	●	●	●	●	●
●			●	●	●	●	●	●	●	●	●	●	●	●	●
●	I,S		●	●	●	●	●	●	●	●	●				●
●	I,S	●	●	●	●	●	●	●	●	●	●	●	●	●	●
●	I,S	●	●	●	●	●	●	●	●	●	●				
●	I,B		●	●	●	●	●								
●	I,B	●	●	●	●	●	●	●	●	●	●	●	●	●	●
●	I,S	●	●	●	●	●	●	●	●	●	●				
●	T,S	●	●												
●	I,S	●	●	●	●	●	●		●	●	●				
●	I,S	●	●	●	●	●	●	●	●	●	●	●	●	●	●
	I,S			●	●	●	●	●	●	●	●	●	●	●	
●		●	●												
●	I,S	●	●	●	●	●	●	●	●	●	●				

Two-Ten and One-Fifty series available in either "Conventional Two-Toning" (top one color, body another color), or in "Special Two-Toning" (top and part of body one color, remainder of body another color).

Opposite page: An interesting offshoot of the '56 Chevy was the El Morocco, built by Detroit industrialist Ruben Allender. He came up with a customized Bel Air ragtop that looked like a scaled down Cadillac Eldorado Biarritz. Only a few were built. (Owner: Glen Warrick) *This page*: What the well dressed Bel Air Sport Coupe (*top*) wore in 1956: bumper and fender guards, stone shields, rocker panel moldings, skirts, and more. (Owner: James E. Watters) The Bel Air two-door sedan (*center and bottom*) listed at $2025. (Owner: Eugene R. Siuda, Jr.)

own name, he went looking for something that sounded a bit like "Eldorado," but not so much as to invite trouble from Cadillac. Ultimately, he picked "El Morocco," and managed to pull a few strings to get the name recognized by the law.

Engineered by Olbrich and professionally crafted, the El Morocco was as much a "junkyard jumble" as any Fifties custom (though the drivetrain was left untouched). Many of the pieces came directly from Allender's warehouse: '37 Dodge headlamp shells reinforced with fiberglass to create the prominent "Dagmar" front bumper guards, a modified Kaiser-Frazer horn button substituting as a hood medallion, "saddle" door-top trim made from '55 Willys dashboard pieces, and '55 Ford

Interior Color and Trim Selections for the 1956 Chevrolet

BEL AIR CONVERTIBLE

Combination No. 602
Ivory Vinyl

Charcoal Gray Pattern Vinyl

Combination No. 621
Tan Vinyl

Copper Pattern Vinyl

BEL AIR BEAUVILLE/NOMAD STATION WAGONS

Combination No. 610/611
Ivory Vinyl

Charcoal Gray Pattern Cloth

Combination No. 619/620
Copper Vinyl

Tan Pattern Cloth

BEL AIR CONVERTIBLE (CUSTOM-COLORED INTERIORS)

Combination No. 607
Light Blue Vinyl

Dark Blue Pattern Vinyl

Combination No. 605
Ivory Vinyl

Red Pattern Vinyl

Combination No. 603
Ivory Vinyl

Dark Turquoise Pattern Vinyl

Combination No. 604
Yellow Vinyl

Charcoal Gray Pattern Vinyl

Combination No. 606
Light Green Vinyl

Dark Green Pattern Vinyl

BEL AIR SPORT SEDAN AND SPORT COUPE (CUSTOM-COLORED INTERIORS)

Combination No. 580
Light Green Vinyl

Dark Green Pattern Cloth

Combination No. 584
Light Turquoise Vinyl

Dark Turquoise Pattern Cloth

Combination No. 581
Light Blue Vinyl

Dark Blue Pattern Cloth

Combination No. 585
Yellow Vinyl

Charcoal Gray Pattern Cloth

Combination No. 583
Red Vinyl

Beige Pattern Cloth

BEL AIR SEDANS

Combination No. 573
Ivory Vinyl

Charcoal Gray Pattern Cloth

Combination No. 617
Tan Vinyl

Copper Pattern Cloth

BEL AIR SPORT SEDAN AND SPORT COUPE

Combination No. 579
Ivory Vinyl

Charcoal Gray Pattern Cloth

Combination No. 618
Copper Vinyl

Tan Pattern Cloth

body moldings fitted to ride atop the fins. The stock Chevy hood ornament was shorn of its wings and given larger Plexiglas fins to mimic the Cadillac mascot, Olbrich's castings faithfully followed 1955-56 Eldorado side trim, and aftermarket wheel covers were chosen to ape Caddy's "Sabre-Spoke" hubcaps. As expected, the major changes showed up at the rear, where a portion of the Chevy fenders was cut away and Eldo-style fiberglass fins were bolted on. Completing the illusion were '55 Dodge taillamps mounted horizontally above dummy exhaust ports.

Though *Motor Trend* predicted "ready acceptance" for the El Morocco, and the fact that it cost about half of what an Eldorado sold for, it still cost about $1000 more than the Chevy on which it was based, and the continental kit with which

Opposite page: This Nassau Blue over Harbor Blue '56 Bel Air Sport Coupe rode a 115-inch wheelbase, as did all '56 Chevys (save Corvettes), and weighed 3222 pounds. *This page*: Chevy offered a half-dozen wagons for 1956, among them the Two-Ten Townsman four-door, six-passenger wagon (*left*). It listed at $2263. The nine-passenger Bel Air Beauville (*top*) was a bit more expensive: $2482.

BEL AIR BEAUVILLE/NOMAD STATION WAGONS (CUSTOM-COLORED INTERIORS)

Combination No. 586/593	Combination No. 587/594 Light Turquoise Vinyl	Combination No. 588/595 Yellow Vinyl	Combination No. 590 Light Green Vinyl	Combination No. 591 Light Blue Vinyl
Red Vinyl				

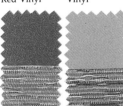

| Beige Pattern Cloth | Dark Turquoise Pattern Cloth | Charcoal Gray Pattern Cloth | Dark Green Pattern Cloth | Dark Blue Pattern Cloth |

TWO-TEN 2-DOOR AND 4-DOOR SEDANS, SPORT COUPE AND SPORT SEDAN

Contemporary Interior Combination No. 564 Starfrost Vinyl	Custom-Colored Interiors Combination No. 565 Starfrost Vinyl	Combination No. 566 Starfrost Vinyl

| Charcoal Gray Pattern Cloth | Dark Green Pattern Cloth | Dark Blue Pattern Cloth |

TWO-TEN DELRAY CLUB COUPE

Contemporary Interior Combination No. 567 Ivory Vinyl	Custom-Colored Interiors Combination No. 568 Ivory Vinyl	Combination No. 569 Ivory Vinyl
Black Vinyl	Dark Green Vinyl	Dark Turquoise Vinyl

BEL AIR SEDANS (CUSTOM-COLORED INTERIORS)

Combination No. 574 Light Green Vinyl	Combination No. 578 Yellow Vinyl	Combination No. 575 Light Blue Vinyl	Combination No. 577 Light Turquoise Vinyl

| Dark Green Pattern Cloth | Charcoal Gray Pattern Cloth | Dark Blue Pattern Cloth | Dark Turquoise Pattern Cloth |

ONE-FIFTY SEDANS

Combination No. 560 Beige, Gold Stripe Vinyl

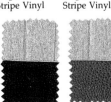

| Black, Gold Dotted Pattern Cloth |

STATION WAGON

Combination No. 616 Beige, Gold Stripe Vinyl	Combination No. 562 Beige, Gold Stripe Vinyl
Charcoal Vinyl	Green Vinyl

TWO-TEN STATION WAGONS

Contemporary Interior Combination No. 609 Starfrost Vinyl	Custom-Colored Combination No. 570 Starfrost Vinyl	Interiors Combination No. 572 Starfrost Vinyl
Charcoal Gray Pattern Vinyl	Dark Green Pattern Vinyl	Dark Turquoise Pattern Vinyl

most were fitted brought the price to around $3400—a lot of money in those days. Makeshift production facilities didn't help, either. In the end, only about 20 '56 El Moroccos were built, 18 ragtops and two hardtops. No matter, the El Morocco would return for 1957 looking even more impressive.

With the "horsepower race" more important than ever in the sales race, Chevy couldn't afford to rest on its '55 laurels, so performance again vied with styling for customer attention in 1956. "The Hot One's Even Hotter," said one ad. "Loves to Go . . . And Looks It!" said another. Actually, Chevy had served notice even before the '56s went on sale. On Labor Day 1955, a heavily disguised Bel Air Sport Sedan charged up Pikes Peak in 17 minutes, 24.05 seconds to set a new American stock-sedan record—fully two minutes, three seconds faster than the previous best.

Driven and prepared by Corvette engineering wizard Zora Arkus-Duntov, this car was powered by the new "Super Turbo-Fire" V-8, available at extra cost on any '56 Chevy. Basically, it was the existing 265 with a special "Power-Pack" kit comprising specific intake manifold, higher-lift camshaft, dual exhausts, four-barrel carburetor, and 9.25:1 compression, Chevy's tightest squeeze yet. Output was a thrilling 205 horsepower at 4600 rpm and 234 pounds/ feet peak torque at the same crank speed, both 14 percent above the '55 powerplant's 180 bhp. Chevy, of course, lost no time in trumpeting its Pikes Peak victory, pointing out that "No other car has ever gone so high so fast—so safely."

But that was only the beginning. Ford upped the power ante at mid-model year, so Chevy made the top Corvette engine an across-the-board passenger-car option. With mechanical instead of hydraulic lifters, the first of the famous "Duntov" cams, plus twin four-barrel carbs, lightweight valves, and larger intake and exhaust passages, it belted out 225 bhp at 5200 rpm.

Opposite page: At $2608, the Nomad was the costliest Chevy for 1956, and perhaps due in good part to the high price it was also the poorest seller. For 1956, it received most of the updates of the regular Chevy line, including the rear wheel cutouts. (Owner: Ken Geiger) *This page*: The '56 Bel Air side trim was modified so that the vertical slash trim followed the slant of the B-pillar. Cargo room was surprisingly generous for such a stylish wagon and the interior was definitely upmarket. (Owner: Ronn Pittman)

Most everyone thinks of the '56 Bel Air Sport Coupe and V-8s as going together, and indeed they did *most* of the time. Note, however, that this particular example (*above*) doesn't have the "V" under the Chevy crest on the hood, meaning that it runs with the 140-horsepower six. (Owner: Jack E. Moore) The bottom-line series continued to be the One-Fifty, but for 1956 it finally got to show off some bodyside trim, which allowed for bodyside two-toning if desired. The four-door sedan (*far left*) listed at $1869; 51,544 were produced. The Two-Ten was a bit fancier, and cost a bit more: $1955 for the four-door sedan (*left*). It was appealing enough that it was the most popular single model in the entire '56 Chevy lineup with 283,125 built.

Tighter 8.0:1 compression made other Chevy V-8s more potent for '56, and wilder cam profiles were ordained for all engines except the two-barrel, 162-bhp mill, which was unchanged but limited to manual transmission. The base Powerglide V-8 now produced 170 bhp at 4400 rpm and a healthy 247 lbs/ft torque at 3300 rpm. All V-8s could be ordered with full-flow (instead of bypass-type) oil filters at extra cost, thanks to minor changes in block casting and oil pan, a reshaped gas tank allowed wagons to be equipped with dual exhausts, which—to reduce noise—had longer mufflers and shorter exhaust pipes than the '55 setup. Warmup and driveability were improved via a revised automatic choke (actually a mid-1955 running change), larger passages for the intake manifold heat riser, and a more deeply grooved throttle body on four-barrel carburetors. Other tweaks included "hotter" four-rib spark plugs and a beefier clutch for Super Turbo-Fire cars, with woven instead of asbestos lining, coil instead of diaphragm pressure-plate spring, and newly vented plate cover.

The old six wasn't ignored either. Now called "Blue Flame 140," it offered that many horses courtesy of 8.0:1 compression, and the hydraulic lifters previously reserved for Powerglide-equipped cars were extended to manual models. Rated torque was up to 210 lbs/ft at 4200 rpm.

To match its more muscular '56 engines, Chevy made several detail chassis revisions in apparent response to criticisms of the '55 models. Longer, lower-rate coil springs appeared up front to reduce nosedive in hard braking, and caster angle was increased one degree for easier steering. The rear leaf springs were mounted two inches further outboard for better cornering stability, and got wider hangers with more rubber to better resist compression from lateral axle motion. Six-leaf (instead of five-leaf) springs were a new option for all models and standard for the Beauville.

These changes were evidently effective, for the '56 Chevy got even better roadability marks than the '55. *Motor Trend's* Jim Lodge rated overall braking as very good, and lauded the "absence of nosedive under all stopping conditions, including panic stops." Handling earned equal praise: "Not only do we admire the steering ease of [the manual system] but believe you will be surprised to find that [the] power steering isn't as noticeable as you might think. . . . Not many things can upset Chevy's composure on the road; it weathers normal rigors with ease. Only when it's

bounced hard by a bump, or rocked into a chuckhole in the midst of a fast turn does it betray its relatively light weight and semi-stiff suspension and skip from its initial track. . . . Recovery from bumps, dips, and potholes is rapid, non-jarring in most cases, and free from wallowing or pitching."

Even so, ride still wasn't the best, though *MT* judged it good. "Not on the soft side, [it] benefits from the car's inherent stability—that is, passengers aren't pitched or rocked from side to side on twisting roads, or see-sawed back and forth in stop-and-go driving. Seats aren't soft either, but they soak up a great deal of chassis movement, level out most minor disturbances."

Not everyone agreed with these assessments. Some testers still thought the ride too hard, and the drum brakes, though good by mid-Fifties standards, wouldn't pass muster today. Other '55 complaints—disappointing interior space, hemmed-in driving position, too few instruments, the manual's clunky column shift—were heard again in '56.

Nobody complained about performance, though. The basic 170-bhp/Powerglide combo zipped from 0-60 mph in 11.9 seconds and topped 98 mph for *Motor Life* testers, while the 205-bhp version recorded 8.9 seconds and 108.7 mph. *Motor Trend* also tried a 205-bhp/Powerglide car and got 10.7 seconds, 109.1 mph flat out, and an 18.3-second standing quarter-mile at 76 mph. Again ordering a lighter-weight Two-Ten two-door, *Road & Track* teamed the 205-bhp V-8 with the stick shift. The results: 0-60 mph in nine seconds flat, 111 mph top speed, and 16.6 seconds at 80 mph in the standing quarter. That was with the stock rear axle, still 3.70:1. Also as before, overdrive cars pulled 4.11:1 gears, those with Powerglide a 3.55:1 final ratio.

Regardless, the Super Turbo-Fire '56 was the fastest Chevy yet and one of the year's quickest production cars at any price. *R&T*, for example, shaved 0.7-second off the 0-60-mph time of its overdrive-equipped '55 (which had the short final drive, of course) and 0.8-second off the quarter-mile clocking. Concluded the editors: "The 14-percent increase in horsepower more than offsets the 10-percent [difference in axle ratios]." *Motor Life* concurred: "The new powerpack [*sic*] was noticeably livelier than last year's 180-bhp job at turnpike speeds. . . . Where the new car should make its biggest showing, 50-80 mph, time was lowered 3.5 seconds from stock '55 time, 0.9-second from the '55 powerpack's 12.9-second time."

And the 225-bhp version was faster still. Tom McCahill drove one, then wrote: "Chevrolet has come up with a poor man's Ferrari. . . . Here's an engine that can wind up tighter than the E string on an East Laplander's mandolin . . . well beyond 6000 rpm without blowing up like a pigeon egg in a shotgun barrel."

So impressed was McCahill that he judged Chevy the year's "best performance buy in the world," while *Motor Life* said it offered the "best performance per dollar." Gushed normally reserved *R&T*: "Without a doubt, the greatest charm of this car is its smooth, quiet-running engine. Even though the compression ratio is extremely high, [we found it] impossible to make it 'ping' on full throttle at any speed. . . . The surge of power (actually torque) is there at all times, and knowing the ultra-short stroke, one gets the impression that this engine would be impossible to 'blow up' even under brutal treatment."

Competition results soon confirmed the road test findings. Smokey Yunick returned to Darlington with a quartet of '56s for a 24-hour enduro; one finished at an average 101.58 mph, beating the previous U.S. production-car record (set by Chrysler) by 11.69 mph. In July, three cars prepared by Vince Piggins, recently recruited from fast-fading Hudson by Chevrolet Engineering, contested the annual Pikes Peak hillclimb. When the dust had settled, Chevy was first, second, fifth, sixth, and 10th. Better yet, winner Jerry Unser, Jr., had leaped to the summit in 16 minutes, 8 seconds, 1:16 faster than Duntov's impressive late-'55 showing. Truly, the "Hot One" *was* even hotter.

It was also safer, though few buyers likely knew it. With an uncharacteristic lack of publicity, GM had standardized so-called "crashproof" door locks in mid-1955. For '56, Chevrolet added dash padding, seatbelts, and even shoulder harnesses as optional extras, again with little fanfare. But while archrival Ford loudly trumpeted its new "Lifeguard" features this year, Chevy peddled mainly performance and styling. And as the sales figures proved, buyers much preferred added dash to a padded dash.

In fact, Chevy's big '56 sales margin over Ford—some 200,000 units for the model year—underscores a curious, but historic, exchange of images between the two old foes. Traditionally, Ford had been the low-price performer, Chevy "old reliable." Now Chevy was "The Hot One" while Ford was seen as safer and more sober, brought about at least in part by an

Although 1956 was a down year for the auto industry, Bel Air soft-top sales kept pace with 1955: 41,268 versus 41,292. The base price was up $138, to $2344, though the wire wheel covers seen on this one (*below*) cost extra. The instrument panel (*above*) now featured small rectangles instead of bowties, and the trunk was roomy. (Owner: Gary Johns)

unexpectedly mild '56 Ford facelift and that celebrated—but ultimately unsuccessful—Lifeguard campaign. The situation would change somewhat for 1957, due to the relative differences between very altered contenders, but that's getting ahead of the story.

In any case, while Ford was pushing safety, Chevy was encouraging its dealers to make use of a "special kit" to tie in with local stock car races. Included were big window posters touting the "Top V-8 in the low-price field" with smaller ones asking people to "Traffic test the short track champ!" and to "Come drive the hot one!" Other exhortations were to "Take the wheel of a winner!" and, in a nod to safety, to "Try performance that puts safety first!" Also part of the package were trunk banners ("56 Chevrolet . . . Watch it go!"), Pace Car door banners, two newspaper ads, two publicity releases, and two radio spots.

Official NASCAR short-track (less than a half-mile in length) standings were also grist for the mill, and for good reason. In

1955, Chevy had won this classification by a sizable margin: 668 points to Oldsmobile's 195, Hudson's 184, Dodge's 176, and Ford's 165. And through April 28, 1956, Chevy was the only make in triple digits: 226 points to second-place Ford's 91. Obviously there was plenty to promote, and Chevy wanted its dealers to blitz the message as loudly as possible: "Chevrolet dealers everywhere benefit from all of the concentrated advertising and promotional activity because it's another way to demonstrate vividly Chevrolet's product superiority."

Options continued to play a big part in Chevy's success, and a few '56 newcomers suggested that "USA-1" was looking upmarket even harder. Besides the aforementioned front seatbelts (a bargain at $10.95) and shoulder harness option (just $9.95), the list now included a Cadillac-style automatic headlamp dimmer ($44.25), remote-control door mirror ($6.95), and rear-mount radio antenna. Air conditioning was still a luxury for most mid-Fifties buyers, but Chevy helped make it less so

by reducing the price of its "Four-Season" system by a sizable $135—though at $430, it was still pretty pricey. Radio choices expanded by one, ranging from $63.50 for the basic manual-tune set to $105 for the pushbutton signal-seeking unit. Power windows and front seat were up $10, to $155, but power steering still cost $92, power brakes $38. Among low-cost miscellany were trunk and underhood lamps at $1.95 each, a $1.60 visor vanity mirror, non-glare rearview mirror at $4.50, and foot-operated or automatic windshield washer ($6.75 and $9.95, respectively).

In all, 1956 was a good year for Chevrolet, even if it was necessarily less spectacular than '55. And it brought a fitting change of leadership, as chief engineer Ed Cole was rewarded for his recent efforts by being named to succeed Tom Keating as division general manager.

One writer accurately summed up '56 as "a year of transition" for Chevrolet. "While the 1956 model did bring a number of firsts . . . it can't compare with the offerings of the previous year or the

More '56 Chevys, like this Bel Air Sport Coupe, probably sport continental tire kits and rear fender skirts these days than when they were new. They are very popular with restorers who feel that these (and other) accessories give their cars a stronger "flavor" of the decade that was the Fifties. Inside, all '56 Chevys carried over the '55 instrument panel with the twin-cowl, fan-shaped nacelles, though the trim was modestly different. Note the full-circle horn ring that came on the Bel Airs. The Powerglide indicator needle was located on the dash just below the speedometer. (Owner: Keefe Habadorn)

succeeding one. . . . With Chevrolet collectors focusing their attention principally on the '55 and '57 models, the '56 is often overlooked. It shouldn't be. It was a vital link [in] the marque's evolution."

And a vital link in the development of the "classic" Chevy, which would reach its peak as it became one of the first collector cars to emerge from this decade. For performance fans and those who appreciate definitive Fifties styling, the best was yet to come

1956 Accessories

All-Weather air conditioning
Fender antenna
Autronic Eye headlamp control
Seatbelts
Self deicing wiper blade
Wiring junction block
Power brakes
Locking gas cap
Continental wheel carrier
Electric clock
Compass
Nylon/plastic/fiber seat covers
Accelerator pedal cover
Wheel covers
Wire wheel covers
Tissue dispenser
Exhaust extension

License plate frame
Glareshades
Fender guards
Tinted safety glass
Door edge guards
Heater and defroster
Vibrator horn
Tool kit
Kool Kooshions
Back-up lamps
Courtesy lamps
Cigarette lighter
Floor mats
Outside rearview mirror
Non-glare rearview mirror
Visor vanity mirror
Body sill moulding
Front fender top moulding
Radio: manual, push-button, or
   signal-seeking

Automatic top raiser (convertible)
Armrests
Safetylight and mirror
Radiator insect screen
Power-positioned front seat
Electric shaver
Door handle shield
Front fender shield
Rear seat speaker
Spotlamp
Power steering
Whitewall tires
Ventshades
Outside visor
Inside visors
Traffic light viewer
Windshield washer (coordinated or
   foot-operated)
Electric-power window lifts
Electric windshield wipers

1956 Chevrolet Specifications, Prices, and Production

Model	Overall Length	Curb Weight	List Price	Production
1956 (115-inch wheelbase)				
ONE-FIFTY				
1502 Sedan, two-door	197.5	3,154	1,826	82,384
1503 Sedan, four-door	197.5	3,196	1,869	51,544
1512 Sedan, utility	197.5	3,117	1,734	9,879
1529 Handyman, two-door wagon	200.8	3,299	2,171	13,487
TWO-TEN				
2102 Sedan, two-door	197.5	3,167	1,912	205,545
2103 Sedan, four-door	197.5	3,202	1,955	283,125
2109 Townsman, four-door wagon	200.8	3,371	2,263	113,656
2113 Sport Sedan, four-door hardtop	197.5	3,252	2,117	20,021
2119 Beauville, four-door wagon (9P)	200.8	3,490	2,348	17,988
2124 Delray, coupe	197.5	3,172	1,971	56,382
2129 Handyman, two-door wagon	200.8	3,334	2,215	22,038
2154 Sport Coupe, hardtop	197.5	3,194	2,063	18,616
BEL AIR				
2402 Sedan, two-door	197.5	3,187	2,025	104,849
2403 Sedan, four-door	197.5	3,221	2,068	269,798
2413 Sport Sedan, four-door hardtop	197.5	3,270	2,230	103,602
2419 Beauville, four-door wagon (9P)	200.8	3,506	2,482	13,279
2429 Nomad, two-door wagon	200.8	3,352	2,608	7,886
2434 Convertible, coupe	197.5	3,330	2,344	41,268
2454 Sport Coupe, hardtop	197.5	3,222	2,176	128,382

Engine/Transmission Availability

	cid	bore/stroke (inches)	compression ratio	bhp @ rpm	carb	trans
1956						
Six	235	3.56 × 3.94	8.0:1	140 @ 4200	1V	3-sp., OD, PG[1]
V-8	265	3.75 × 3.00	8.0:1	162 @ 4200	2V	3-sp., OD
V-8	265	3.75 × 3.00	8.0:1	170 @ 4400	2V	PG[1]
V-8	265	3.75 × 3.00	8.0:1	205 @ 4600	4V	3-sp., OD, PG[1]
V-8	265	3.75 × 3.00	9.25:1	225 @ 5200	2-4V	3-sp., OD, PG[1]

[1]Powerglide

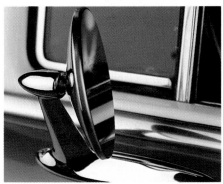

1957

THE ULTIMATE "CLASSIC" CHEVY

The road isn't built that can make it breathe hard!

Curves don't come too sharp or hills too steep for this nimble new Chevy. It's sweet, smooth and sassy with new velvety V8 power, new roadability, a new ride and everything it takes to make you the relaxed master of any road you travel.

Bring on the mountains! This new Chevy takes steep grades with such an easy-going stride you hardly even give them a thought. There's horsepower aplenty tucked away under that hood—the Chevy kind, just rarin' to handle any hill you aim it at.

And no matter how curvy the road may be, a light touch keeps Chevrolet right on course. You'll like the solid way it stays put on sharp turns.

A car has to have a special kind of build to handle and ride and run like a Chevy. It has to have Chevrolet's low, wide stance, its outrigger type rear springs and well-balanced weight distribution, with the pounds in the right places. Try one soon at your Chevrolet dealer's. . . . Chevrolet Division of General Motors, Detroit 2, Michigan.

More beautifully built and shows it—the new Chevrolet with Body by Fisher.

Chevy touted its '57s as "Sweet, Smooth, and Sassy!" And indeed, the new styling *was* sweet, the finest of the 1955-57 "classic" Chevys; the new Turboglide transmission was "as smooth as velvet underpants"; and the new fuel-injected 283 V-8 was *very* sassy!

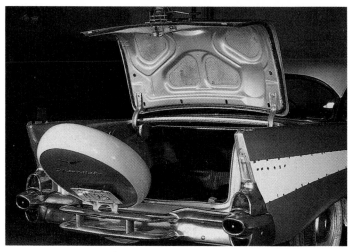

F ord and Plymouth both boasted all-new styling for 1957, and they were bigger and more powerful as well. Chevy, meanwhile, had to make do with a facelift of its 1955 bodyshell, but that didn't mean that GM's largest division was standing still. On the contrary, Chevy received a major refreshening style-wise for 1957 and some important engineering upgrades, including a big boost in horsepower. The ads proclaimed that "This is the car that's fresher and friskier from its own special look to its new Ramjet fuel injection!"

Of course, a facelift and more horsepower don't necessarily make a great automobile—unless it's the '57 Chevrolet. Almost from the day production ceased, it's been coveted not only as the last of the "classic" Chevys, but the best—the definitive example of *Automobilis Americanis* in the fabulous Fifties. In fact, except for its Corvette cousins and Ford's two-seater 1955-57 Thunderbirds, it remains the most collectible car of the decade.

In a way, this enduring adoration is difficult to fathom. Much of it stems from the undeniable performance of the newly enlarged, 283-cubic-inch V-8, and the presumed historical significance of the top 283-horsepower version with "Ramjet" fuel injection, which was of course also available on the '57 Corvette. Needless to say, it was this development that prompted Chevrolet to claim an industry first in that now-famous ad headlined "1 h.p. per cubic inch." "Chevy attains the engineer's dream. . ." the ad read. "Every competitive field has certain magic milestones. In track, the four-minute mile. In aviation, the sound barrier. In mountain climbing, the ascent of Everest . . . and so on. In American automobile engineering, the magic milestone is this: *one horsepower from every cubic inch of engine displacement!* Chevrolet is the first American production car to achieve this goal; from our 283-cubic-inch V8, with fuel injection and 10.5 to 1 compression ratio, we pull 283 h.p. Naturally, we're proud. Because this is proof, in cold figures, of the *extra* efficiency of Chevrolet's advanced valve gear, free-breathing manifolding and ultra-short stroke."

All well and good, except that Chevy, Chevy partisans, and most historians have long overlooked some salient facts. First, Chrysler had already achieved this engineering milepost the previous season and *without* such exotica—just optional high-compression heads that gave its 354-cubic-inch Hemi V-8 a rated 355 bhp in the 300-B. Second, Chevy wasn't alone with a '57 "fuelie." Pontiac introduced a similar setup with its flashy, mid-year Bonneville convertible, and the Bendix "Electrojector" system was available—if rarely seen—from Plymouth, Dodge, DeSoto, Chrysler, and even Rambler. Moreover, Ramjet was as expensive as any of its ilk and just as troublesome, at least initially, so it was just as short-lived, at least in the bread-and-butter Chevys.

But credit where credit is due. The Bonneville and high-performance MoPars were expensive rarities, while the costliest '57 Chevy—a Bel Air Nomad with everything, *including* Ramjet—sold for thousands less. Then, too, only Chevy offered

Opposite page: The front end design of the '57 Chevy in progress: May 3, 1954 (*top left*), August 3, 1955 (*top right*), and an almost finalized (undated) mock-up (*bottom left*). Note the exhaust outlets at the bottom extremes of the bumper (*bottom right*). *This page:* The design of the '57 is nearly locked in: One-Fifty side trim and fender skirts (*top left*), two-toning that was rejected (*top right*), and some interior proposals (*left*).

a "fuelie" on *all* of its '57 models, right down to the cheap and lightweight One-Fifty utility sedan. Yet you really didn't need it. Even in carbureted form, the 283 packed more power than the hottest '56 setup. And since this year's all-new Ford and Plymouth were both larger and heavier, Chevy continued to enjoy a substantial performance edge not just in the low-price field, but industry-wide.

Which brings up another part of the '57's appeal, namely what Chevrolet became for '58: bigger, heavier, thirstier; slower, costlier, less agile; and more Buick-like in ride, appearance, and appointments. Yet the '58s sold relatively *better* than the '57s despite a much more difficult market.

Why? Because 1957 was not the banner year Detroit expected, and competition was fiercer than ever. Though total car/truck volume was up somewhat from '56, car output actually declined by nearly 85,000 units to just over 6.2 million, due partly to the start of a national economic recession that would devastate the '58 market. Styling again proved the deciding

sales factor, and General Motors lost ground, from 52.8 to 46.1 percent in market share, by inexplicably losing its traditional industry design leadership, mostly to Virgil Exner's striking new Chrysler Corporation fleet. Against those cars and George Walker's equally new Ford and Mercury, the rebodied '57 Cadillac, Buick, and Oldsmobile seemed dull and conservative (bloated, even), while Chevrolet and Pontiac wore only third-season facelifts.

Almost predictably, then, Ford outpaced Chevy in model year production by some 170,000 cars, Plymouth wrested third place back from Buick, Mercury and Dodge pressed Pontiac, and DeSoto and Chrysler closed in on Cadillac. Chevy's one consolation was nipping Ford in calendar year output (which included a lot of '58s) and total market share, albeit by razor-thin margins: 128 units and 0.01 percent (24.90 to 24.89), respectively. With all this, *Motor Life* magazine was devastatingly accurate in assessing the '57 Chevy: "Never before has it had so much to offer.

And as a matter of fact, never has it needed it more."

More was certainly Chevy's watchword this year. The big news, of course, was the 283 V-8, created by opening up the 265's bore by 0.11 inch to 3.88 inches (stroke remained at 3.00 inches). It arrived in no fewer than six versions—two fuelies and four with carburetors—swelling engine choices from five to eight.

The familiar two-barrel, 162-bhp 265 continued as the base V-8 with manual shift, but the mildest 283—also called Turbo-Fire—was now its automatic counterpart, sporting a single four-barrel carburetor, 8.5:1 compression, and 185 bhp at 4600 rpm. Then came a Super Turbo-Fire quintet with 9.5:1 compression on all but the 283-bhp fuelie. The single four-barrel version yielded 220 bhp at 4800 rpm. Twin quads boosted that to either 245 bhp at 5000 rpm or 270 at 6000 rpm, the former available with any transmission, the latter a high-lift-camshaft version limited to a close-ratio three-speed manual. Fuel injection outputs were 250

Ford (*center*) and Plymouth (*bottom*) were all-new for 1957, giving them a sales advantage over the facelifted Chevy (*top*). And indeed, Ford outsold Chevy, while Plymouth gained ground. The models shown are the Chevy Bel Air Sport Coupe (Owners: Ron and Linda Jeurgens, left, and Jim Van Gondon), Ford Fairlane 500 four-door Victoria (Owner: Lee Willet), and Plymouth Fury (Owner: Bob Schmidt).

bhp at 5000 rpm or, on 10.5:1 compression, 283 bhp at 6200 rpm; again, the latter was a high-lift-cam unit available only with the three-speed.

Regardless of power rating, all '57 Chevy V-8s featured a number of internal changes. Longer-reach spark plugs brought metal deflection shields to protect wiring and plug caps from manifold heat, while upper blocks employed thicker castings to prevent cylinder wall distortion from overtightening of the hold-down bolts.

Fuel passages were newly tapered, increasing in cross section toward the intake ports and in the "ram's horn" exhaust manifold for improved scavenging and volumetric efficiency. And there were new carburetor fuel filters, larger ports, wider main bearings, stainless-steel expanders for piston oil-control rings, and a choke relocated to improve hot starting. Dual-exhaust engines now got a balance tube that equalized flow so that both mufflers would have approximately the same service life.

The six-cylinder "Blue Flame 140" returned with a more compact air cleaner trainer on the carburetor inlet to supplement the gas tank filter, thus reducing the chances of stalling due to clogging from foreign matter.

Chassis changes began with updated electrics across-the-board: relocated battery and voltage regulator, line fuses for lamp

circuits in cars without the accessory junction box, a chassis wiring harness with separate units connected by multi-plugs, and a new distributor for V-8s. High-torque clutches were specified for all powerteams save manual-shift 283s with injection or twin four-barrel carbs, where a new semi-centrifugal unit was adopted. Fuel economy considerations prompted higher (numerically lower) final drive ratios for all but the optional stick/overdrive transmission, which remained at 4.11:1. The manual three-speed now drove through a standard 3.55:1 gearset (the previous 3.70 cog was optional), while the automatic ratio was now 3.34:1 instead of 3.55:1.

As elsewhere in the industry this year, Chevy switched from 15- to 14-inch wheels and fitted low-pressure tires, reducing overall height 0.4- to 0.7-inch depending on model. Width and wheelbase went unchanged, but overall length was now 200 inches across the board, so the frame was strengthened with new front braces. Shocks were also revised to match the heavier bodies, power control-arm ball-joint and seal assemblies were adopted for the front suspension, and rear springs were again moved a bit further outboard for handling stability. Front brakes were treated to new heat-resistant linings and stiffer pull-back springs on secondary shoes.

"The biggest auto news of 1957" was Ramjet fuel injection, manufactured by GM's Rochester carburetor division and developed by John Dolza, E.A. Kehoe, Donald Stoltman, and Corvette chief engineer Zora Arkus-Duntov. A mechanical system, it was what we'd now call a continuous-flow multi-point system, with a separate injector for each cylinder, plus special fuel meter, manifold assembly, and air meter replacing the normal carburetor and intake manifold.

Chevy's 1957 dealer sales book described Ramjet's operation as follows: "The basic principle of fuel injection is to deliver fuel directly to [the] cylinder in just the right amount and under precisely controlled conditions. . . . [The injectors, or nozzles] atomize the gasoline, aiming it directly at the intake ports in a pressurized spray. The amount of fuel delivered depends on the air flow, which in turn is controlled by the accelerator. Outside air . . . flows through a special chamber which divides into separate tubes, called ram tubes, one leading to each cylinder. As the air approaches the cylinder, it mixes with fuel being continuously sprayed from the nozzle, carrying the atomized fuel directly into the cylinder in a precisely controlled air/fuel ratio. [A] fuel pump delivers fuel to each nozzle by a pressurizing pump from the fuel reservoir through a regulating system that meters it to the cylinders." A special two-piece aluminum manifold casting carried the air passages and air/fuel metering bases in its upper half, while the lower contained the ram tubes and covered the top center of the engine.

Ramjet was touted as having several advantages: "increased power, instant accelerator response, faster cold starts, smoother engine warmup, elimination of carburetor icing . . . and *better* overall fuel economy." Volumetric efficiency was undoubtedly superior, fuelies having about five more horsepower than a comparable twin-four-barrel engine with no other changes. As there was no carburetor, Chevy also claimed that FI reduced stalling tendencies from momentary fuel starva-

Chevy listed four hardtops for 1957, the most popular being the two-door Bel Air Sport Coupe (*top*), of which 166,426 were built. At the bottom of the Chevy lineup was the One-Fifty series. It was comprised of four models: four-door sedan, Handyman two-door wagon, and the two-door sedan and Utility sedan. The last two looked alike from the exterior. Listing at $1996 and $1885, respectively, they enjoyed a production run of 79,074 units.

tion. To handle their extra power, fuelies got mechanical instead of hydraulic lifters, thicker front and intermediate main bearings (by 0.063-inch), and a special distributor with breaker points directly above the shaft bearing to help reduce gap fluctuations.

Chevy's other big engineering news for '57 was a second automatic transmission. Called Turboglide, it arrived after the beginning of the model year as a $231

option for any 283 V-8 save the 270- and 283-bhp versions, and weighed 82 pounds less than the familiar Powerglide, which was priced at $188. The work of engineers Oliver Kelly and Frank Winchell, it was a two-speed, five-element geared-converter type modeled after Buick's famous Dynaflow, with three turbines and twin planetary gearsets plus variable-pitch stator and a conventional torque-converter pump. Chevy had a more appealing way to put it:

"...and now Turboglide, a torque converter with Triple-Turbine take-off and a Hill Retarder for greatly increased 'slowing power' on grades!" It was also claimed to be "...the first and only triple-turbine transmission."

Turboglide sent power to the driveshaft via turbine rotation through the converter pump's oil supply. Differing vane angles determined which turbines rotated when. Decreasing turning force or torque from the first turbine brought the second into play, which drove its shaft and the output shaft through the rear planetary gearset and on to the third turbine. Ultimately, all three freewheeled as the car gathered speed. Flooring the accelerator activated a kickdown feature that increased stator pitch for increased torque to the output shaft. Turboglide also incorporated a "Hill Retarder" (indicated by "HR" on the shift quadrant) that helped slow the car on steep descents by inducing drag on the rear wheels via turbulence in the converter-pump oil.

Unfortunately, Turboglide's complexity proved a nightmare for both customers and mechanics: prone to failure, and difficult and expensive to repair. Too bad, because according to *Mechanix Illustrated's* Tom McCahill, it was "as smooth as velvet underpants" when working properly. Years later, Chevy engineer Vince Piggins opined that "there was very little need of another transmission, and it was expensive to build." After persisting with it through 1961, Chevy reverted to Powerglide alone through 1965, then added the more reliable Turbo Hydra-Matic already used by sister GM divisions. Said Piggins: "It would have taken a few more years to really get Turboglide to the reliability stage that Hydra-Matic had already achieved, and sales being what they were, it just didn't make sense."

Though Chevy's '57 engineering changes were extensive, they were expected in the Fifties, when sales considerations dictated expansive—and thus expensive—makeovers for the last year of an existing design. Styling was even more important to sales and thus got even more attention, so Chevy again received a substantial and costly facelift, even though a complete redesign was scheduled for '58.

Part of this reflected Chevy's awareness of the all-new '57 Ford and Plymouth, though they actually affected 1958-59 developments more than '57 styling. But as former studio head Clare MacKichan

later observed: "We just had no choice [but] to carry the line out until 1958, [so we] were as extreme as we could be while saving the deck, roof, and doors. Those were the established ground rules. [Yet] there was a great deal of pressure on us [to add distinction] to the '57."

They succeeded by invoking ideas tried long before, with the result being touted as "BOLD 'BIG CAR' STYLING!" plus the added—and exaggerated—assertion that "...Chevy has the boldest, biggest look in the low-price field!" But even though Chevrolet was smaller than the competition this year, the styling was deliberately

fashioned to make it *look* as large as possible. The '57's massive new bumper/grille, for example, had been evident in various sketches since 1949, and one 1953 Carl Renner rendering was surprisingly close to the eventual production design. High cost—and styling chief Harley Earl's wishes—precluded it on the '55, but a sizable budget made it possible for '57, "when they [finally] had money to do something quite radical for Chevrolet," as Renner recalled.

Not that the stylists worried about money. "I think today there's a little more awareness of that," MacKichan told

Opposite page: As since 1953, the best selling model in the Bel Air lineup was the four door sedan, which listed at $2290 in 1957. Output was a substantial 254,331 units, though this was down from 269,798 in 1956 and 345,372 in 1955. (Owner: Wayne Rife) *This page*: All 1957 Chevys could be ordered with Ramjet fuel injection, even the lowly One-Fifty Utility Sedan (*above*), which at 3163 pounds was the lightest model in the line. This particular car is called the "Black Widow" and carries FI badges on the rear fenders. (Owner: Robert L. Walden) By comparison, the Bel Air Sport Coupe (*left*) weighed in at 3278 pounds. (Courtesy of Capitol Corvette & Classic Cars)

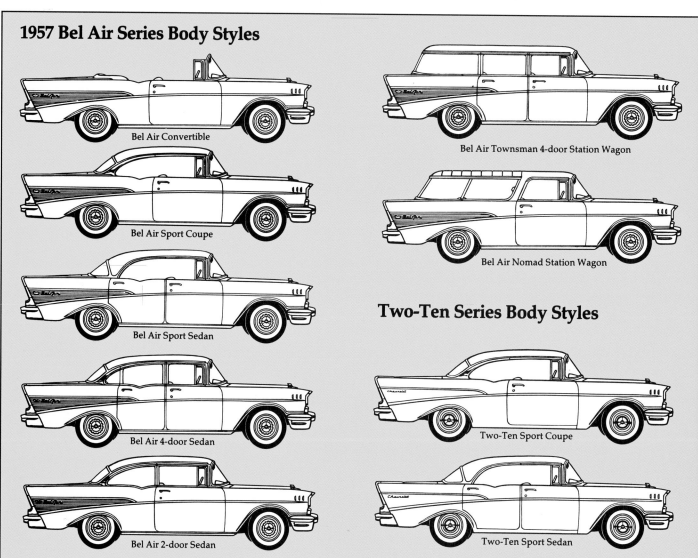

1957 Bel Air Series Body Styles

Bel Air Convertible

Bel Air Sport Coupe

Bel Air Sport Sedan

Bel Air 4-door Sedan

Bel Air 2-door Sedan

Bel Air Townsman 4-door Station Wagon

Bel Air Nomad Station Wagon

Two-Ten Series Body Styles

Two-Ten Sport Coupe

Two-Ten Sport Sedan

The Chevy four-door Sport Sedan was in its second year in 1957. This year it retailed for $2364, up $134 from 1956. No matter, buyers liked the four-door hardtops enough to drive 137,672 of the '57s home, an increase of 34,070 over inaugural 1956. Like all '57 Chevys, the Sport Sedan rode a 115-inch wheelbase and measured 200 inches overall. This compared with 116- and 118-inch wheelbases for the all-new '57 Fords, which stretched from 201.6-207.7 inches overall. Likewise, the equally all-new '57 Plymouth was larger: 118-inch wheelbase (122 for wagons), 204.6-208.6 inches overall. At 3340 pounds, the Sport Sedan was the heaviest '57 Chevy, excluding wagons and the convertible. (Owner: Bill Bodnarchuk)

Collectible Automobile® magazine in 1984. "But at that time, chief designers didn't have that under their wings. There would be much direction from Chevrolet Division . . . and Earl would pass down statements on whether we were getting into trouble. But other than that, we didn't concern ourselves. Our main thing was to get the design right."

Reflecting on his classic Chevy efforts, MacKichan told *CA* that there wasn't much "continuity in thinking" from one year to the next. But as the '56 facelift had evolved from stillborn '55 ideas, "some of the ideas we worked on for the '56 [showed] up on the '57. I think by the time we got to [that] the feeling for exterior ornamentation was even stronger. . . . Amazingly, Harley Earl liked [the Bel Air's anodized aluminum bodyside] panels very much, whereas with the '55 he wanted a very clean car."

Chevy's '57 facelift was carefully detailed for a longer, lower look, which, as men-tioned, wasn't entirely illusion. Cowl height was reduced with a new ventilation system featuring fresh-air intakes in the headlamp eyebrows feeding long, concealed ducts to the interior, one of the car's more radical features. This led to a lower hood, with twin "lance-shaped windsplits" instead of a central ornament. The new bumper/grille was dominated by a thick horizontal bar with a large Chevy crest in the center and small, circular parking lamps at each end, set against a fine mesh background. The bumper was scooped into a wide U, then flared up and out into bomb-like guards at the grille extremities. These were normally flat-faced, but could be fitted with optional black-rubber tips. It all added up to a fully fresh face, more massive and bearing more than a passing resemblance to Cadillac. While stylists deemed it "heavy" next to 1955-56 appearance, Chevy, for its part, bragged about the result as "unified bumper and grille styling."

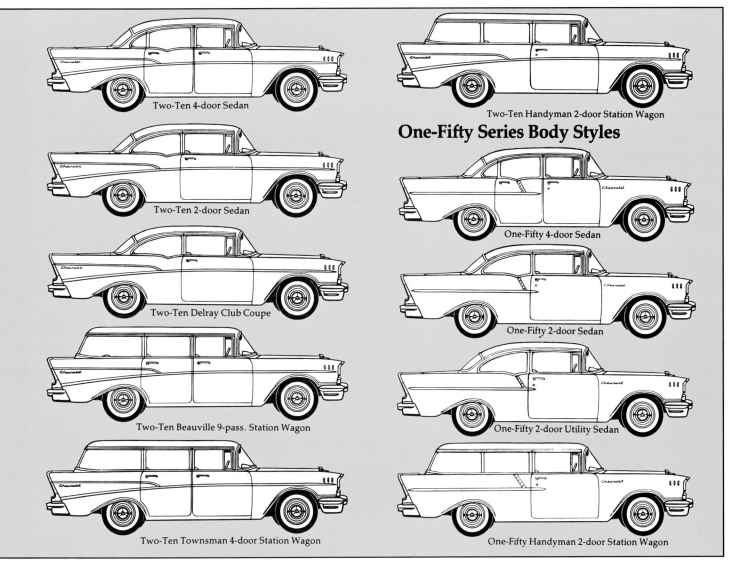

Two-Ten 4-door Sedan

Two-Ten 2-door Sedan

Two-Ten Delray Club Coupe

Two-Ten Beauville 9-pass. Station Wagon

Two-Ten Townsman 4-door Station Wagon

Two-Ten Handyman 2-door Station Wagon

One-Fifty Series Body Styles

One-Fifty 4-door Sedan

One-Fifty 2-door Sedan

One-Fifty 2-door Utility Sedan

One-Fifty Handyman 2-door Station Wagon

Elsewhere, the '57 not only looked different than the '56 but, to most eyes, *better*. Bodyside trim was adroitly handled. One-Fiftys continued with a short vertical "slash" molding at the beltline dip, meeting a half-length horizontal bar running back along the upper flanks. Two-Tens wore a sloping full-length strip that split just aft of the notch into a wedge, painted to match the roof color on two-tone cars. Bel Airs got the same, but filled the wedge with brushed aluminum, one of Harley Earl's favorite materials. The decision to give Two-Tens the upper molding that defined the wedge apparently came very late, as some early press pictures showed just the single full-length strip, two-toned below to match the roof.

Out back were reshaped fenders incorporating exceedingly modest blade fins to accentuate the lower front end—and keep up with the competition. Taillamps took the form of a half-moon at the base of each fin just above the bumper, which jutted out into oval pods for the optional backup lamps. Directly below were inverted half-moons painted black. These were intended for the backup lamps, as stylists had wanted to route the exhausts through the bumper pods. But a similar treatment had caused soot deposits on the '56 Corvette (and on other makes that had tried it), so the backup lamps were moved up, their original housings filled in, and exhaust tips placed below the bumper. The '56's concealed fuel filler returned as a side-hinged panel in the left fin's vertical edge molding, just above the taillamp.

Inside was a new asymmetrical "Command Post" dashboard (also sometimes called "Flight Panel"), with a raised cluster ahead of the steering wheel housing a large, circular speedometer between smaller-diameter water temperature and fuel gauges. Minor switchgear was arrayed below. Radios were still mounted centrally, above the glovebox, but the front speaker now faced upward from the middle of the dash top instead of directly at the right front passenger, and the panel was slightly concave all the way across instead of flat. Revised seat and door panel trim gave Two-Tens patterned cloth and vinyl (all vinyl on the Del Ray club coupe). Vinyl and loomed Jacquard cloth dressed Bel Airs, which also featured full carpeting as standard.

The '57 Chevy's even more Cadillac-like styling was encouragement enough for Ruben Allender to continue with the El Morocco he had first brought out in 1956. This year's edition flaunted styling cues

from all three Eldorados: Biarritz, Seville, and the new flagship Brougham. Borrowed from the Biarritz/Seville were the "shark" fins and single headlights (versus the Brougham's stepped fins and quad lights), while the L-shaped bodyside moldings and broad appliques on the lower rear-quarters were more akin to the $13,000 Brougham. The grillework was an Eldo-like aluminum latticework affair, sans the Chevy's grille bar, so the parking lights were moved down to the otherwise stock front bumper. Other touches included turbine-type or "spinner" wheels covers and a leather pad on the steering wheel hub. Deeply stamped into the latter were the words "El Morocco Custom Built For. . . ." As before, there were no mechanical or structural changes from the stock Chevys, although the '57 El Moroccos were based on the Two-Ten two-

Among the "classic" 1955-57 Chevy ragtops, the '57 Bel Air convertible was the most plentiful—a fact that hasn't gone unnoticed by grateful collectors. That year production totaled 47,562 units, up from 41,292 and 41,268 in 1955 and '56, respectively. Of course, the price was up, too, to $2511. This put it $167 over the '56 model, and made it the most expensive non-wagon in the entire '57 Chevy lineup. It was also the heaviest non-wagon model: 3409 pounds. This Matador Red soft-top sports the optional simulated knock-off "wheel spinner" hubcaps and the black rubber, "Dagmar"-like front bumper cushions. (Owners: Roger and Betty Jerie)

and four-door hardtops and the Bel Air convertible. Alas, only about 16 '57s had been produced by early 1957, after which the El Morocco disappeared forever.

The '57 Chevrolet options sheet read much like the '56 edition except for Turboglide, the new engines, and generally lower prices. For example, power steering was now $70, down $22, and air conditioning was $5 less at $425, though power brakes were up $12 to $54. Power windows cost $59 for two-doors and $102 on four-door models, while the power seat came in at $43. Not surprisingly, Ford downplayed its Lifeguard safety features this season, but Chevy continued to list seatbelts and shoulder harnesses along with the usual extra-cost knickknacks, such as "Kool Kooshins," radiator insect screen, "traffic light viewer" (a small convex lens mounted at the top of the dashboard in front of the driver), electric or foot-pump windshield washer, spinners for the optional full-disc wheel covers, and a new tri-tone horn. Missing was the convertible's "automatic top raiser."

Bowing on October 17, 1956, the '57 Chevy lineup again listed 19 models in the three familiar series. The one model change was a six-passenger Bel Air Townsman wagon replacing the nine-passenger Beauville. Alas, the beautiful Nomad was in its farewell season as a distinctively styled "hardtop" wagon. Only 6103 would be built, the lowest figure for its three-year production run. Trim was again stock Bel Air except for Nomad script and a small gold "V" on V-8 tailgates.

Chevy ads aptly described the '57s as "Sweet, Smooth, and Sassy!" Others went into more detail: "sweet (just look!) smooth (ah, that Turboglide!) sassy (just drive it!)." And despite this year's more muscular

This page: "There's horsepower aplenty tucked away under that hood—the Chevy kind, just rarin' to handle any hill you aim it at." Even allowing for advertising hyperbole, this wasn't just idle boasting on Chevy's part, for 1957 was the year that the high-stepping Turbo-Fire 265 V-8 was opened up to 283 cubic inches. That upped horsepower to 185 or 220 horsepower with a two- and four-barrel carburetor, or 245 and 270 bhp with dual quads. The big news, however, was the new Rochester Ramjet fuel injection, which upped the ante to 250 and 283 strong and eager horses. *Opposite page:* Aside from the convertible, the Bel Air Sport Coupe was the sportiest of the 1957 Chevys. Like all Bel Airs, it flaunted a silver anodized aluminum insert on its rear flanks. Listing at $2299, the Sport Coupe weighed 3278 pounds. (Owner: Bill Bodnarchuk)

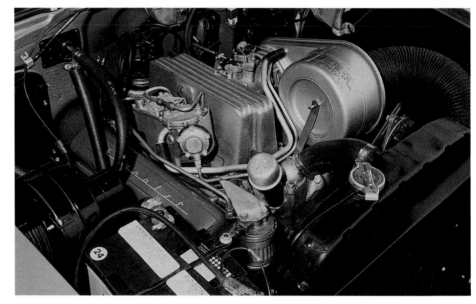

Solid Colors for the 1957 Chevrolet

Onyx Black	Inca Silver	Imperial Ivory	Matador Red
Harbor Blue	Larkspur Blue	Tropical Turquoise	Surf Green
Highland Green	Colonial Cream	Coronado Yellow	Canyon Coral
Sierra Gold	Adobe Beige	Dusk Pearl	Laurel Green

Two-Tone Combinations

Onyx Black / India Ivory	Imperial Ivory / Inca Silver	Larkspur Blue / Harbor Blue	India Ivory / Larkspur Blue
India Ivory / Tropical Turquoise	Surf Green / Highland Green	India Ivory / Surf Green	India Ivory / Coronado Yellow
Onyx Black / Colonial Cream	India Ivory / Colonial Cream	India Ivory / Canyon Coral	Adobe Beige / Sierra Gold
India Ivory / Matador Red	Colonial Cream / Laurel Green	Imperial Ivory / Dusk Pearl	

Fords and Plymouths, "The Hotter One," as *Motor Trend* called it, remained the hottest of the low-price three. Even the base 283/Powerglide combo was capable of 11-second 0-60-mph acceleration. Walt Woron's 220-bhp/Turboglide car easily topped 100 mph, hit 60 mph from rest in 10.1 seconds, and scampered from 50 to 80 mph in 10 seconds. "Appreciably faster on all counts," wrote Woron, who praised the

1957 COLORS	Bel-Air		
	2-door Sedan	4-door Sedan	Sport Sedan
SOLID COLORS			
Onyx Black	●	●	●
Inca Silver	●	●	●
Imperial Ivory	●	●	●
Matador Red	●	●	●
Harbor Blue	●	●	●
Larkspur Blue	●	●	●
Tropical Turquoise	●	●	●
Surf Green	●	●	●
Highland Green	●	●	●
Colonial Cream	●	●	●
Coronado Yellow			
Canyon Coral			
Sierra Gold	●	●	●
Adobe Beige	●	●	●
Dusk Pearl			
Laurel Green			
TWO-TONE			
Onyx Black / India Ivory	●	●	●
Imperial Ivory / Inca Silver	●	●	●
Larkspur Blue / Harbor Blue	●	●	●
India Ivory / Larkspur Blue	●	●	●
India Ivory / Tropical Turquoise	●	●	●
Surf Green / Highland Green	●	●	●
India Ivory / Surf Green	●	●	●
India Ivory / Coronado Yellow	●	●	●
Onyx Black / Colonial Cream	●	●	●
India Ivory / Colonial Cream	●	●	●
India Ivory / Canyon Coral	●	●	●
Adobe Beige / Sierra Gold	●	●	●
India Ivory / Matador Red	●	●	●
Colonial Cream / Laurel Green	●	●	●
Imperial Ivory / Dusk Pearl	●	●	●

new Turboglide for its near imperceptible shift action and fine engine braking.

Later in the year, *MT* tested a Powerglide-equipped 270-bhp Bel Air Sport Sedan for a Chevy/Ford/Plymouth showdown. It clocked 9.9 seconds for the 0-60-mph sprint and 17.5 seconds at 77.5 mph in the standing quarter-mile. Scribbler Pete Molson termed these figures "impressive, particularly when you remember that we had a low-performance transmission. It beat all the times of last year's powerpacked [sic] test car and all the times of the Ford and Plymouth this year except for the Plymouth's time from 0-45 mph."

All was not perfect, of course. Molson disliked the '57's "somewhat softer ride, with resultant greater lean on corners and less confidence for the driver. There is no question that the car looks and feels bigger. . . . We prefer the taut feel of the '56. . . . Front-end heaviness is evident in a mushier feel [though] Chevrolet has the best weight distribution among the three cars. . . . Normal highway dips cause it no embarrassment. When they get bad, it bounces (but doesn't bottom) and then recovers quickly with no oscillation. . . ." *MT* also criticized early brake fade, but liked the new dash and continued to laud Chevy's

Exterior Color Selections for the 1957 Chevrolet

Sport Coupe	Convertible	Townsman 6-pass. Wagon	Nomad	Two-Ten 2-door Sedan	Two-Ten 4-door Sedan	Two-Ten Sport Sedan	Two-Ten Sport Coupe	Delray Club Coupe	Beauville 9-pass. Wagon	Townsman 4-door Wagon	Handyman 2-door Wagon	One-Fifty 2-door Sedan	One-Fifty 4-door Sedan	Utility Sedan	Handyman 2-door Wagon
●	A	●	●	●	●	●	●	●	●	●	●	●	●	●	●
●	A	●	●	●	●	●	●	●	●	●	●				
●	A	●	●	●	●	●	●	●	●	●	●	●	●	●	●
●	A	●	●	●	●	●	●	●	●	●	●	●	●	●	●
●	B	●	●	●	●	●	●	●	●	●	●	●	●	●	●
●	B	●	●	●	●	●	●	●	●	●	●	●	●	●	●
●	A	●	●	●	●	●	●	●	●	●	●	●	●	●	●
●	C	●	●	●	●	●	●	●	●	●	●	●	●	●	●
●	C	●	●	●	●	●	●	●	●	●	●	●	●	●	●
●	A	●	●	●	●	●	●	●	●	●	●	●	●	●	●
	A														
	A														
●	D	●	●					●	●	●	●				
●	D	●	●	●	●	●	●	●	●	●	●	●	●	●	●
	A														
	A														
●		●	●	●	●	●	●	●	●	●	●	●	●	●	●
●	n	●	●	●	●	●	●	●	●	●	●	●	●	●	●
●	o	●	●	●	●	●	●	●	●	●	●	●	●	●	●
●		●	●	●	●	●	●	●	●	●	●	●	●	●	●
●	t	●	●	●	●	●	●	●	●	●	●	●	●	●	●
●	w	●	●	●	●	●	●	●	●	●	●	●	●	●	●
●	o	●	●	●	●	●	●	●	●	●	●	●	●	●	●
●	-	●	●	●	●	●	●	●	●	●	●	●	●	●	●
●	t	●	●	●	●	●	●	●	●	●	●	●	●	●	●
●	o	●	●	●	●	●	●	●	●	●	●	●	●	●	●
●	n	●	●	●	●	●	●	●	●	●	●	●	●	●	●
●	i	●	●					●	●	●	●				
●	n	●	●	●	●	●	●	●	●	●	●	●	●	●	●
●	g	●	●	●	●	●	●	●	●	●	●	●	●	●	●
●		●	●	●	●	●	●	●	●	●	●	●	●	●	●

Convertible Top Colors: A-Ivory or Black; B-Ivory or Light Blue; C-Ivory or Medium Green; D-Ivory or Beige

Chevy, like other automakers, continually compared its own cars to those of its rivals. Seen here (*top row*) is a September 26, 1956 side-by-side comparison of the '57 Ford Fairlane 500 and the Chevy Bel Air. The Ford looks marginally wider and lower, as indeed it was, but the '57 Chevrolet was deliberately styled—successfully, one could argue—to make it look larger than it really was. Pick *your* favorite. The Bel Air, here the convertible (*left*), had a bit of a Cadillac "look" about it. (Owner: Bill Bodnarchuk)

easy steering and superior workmanship. The last point was telling, as the '57 Plymouth and, to a lesser degree, the Ford were rust prone, and both suffered from all too frequent lapses in workmanship.

The fuelies promised to be the fastest regular Chevys, but few knew for sure because Ramjet was a very rare commodity. One reason was price. At $550, it was prohibitively expensive as a family-car option, especially one whose merits even the experts debated. (FI was still a strange novelty at the time.) Accordingly, it disappeared as a passenger-car option after 1958. Another problem, ironically enough, was its early announcement, which touched off a sudden demand for injectors from its sister GM divisions and even other automakers that limited Chevy's own supply and thus fuelie installations. Sometimes, it doesn't pay to be first.

Thus, only a few hundred Ramjet engines were installed in the regular Chevys for '57, and they weren't that common in Corvettes, either. But as would be expected, most ended up in the 'Vettes, where the option not only made more sense but was more palatable, given the two-seater's higher base price and more prosperous clientele. According to *MT*'s Woron, the sports car did 0-60 mph in a swift 7.2 seconds with the 250-bhp engine and stickshift, while the 283-bhp version easily exceeded 134 mph. With the latter engine, suitable gearing, and some 400 pounds more weight, a standard '57 two-door might have done 0-60 mph in about 8.0 seconds and 120 mph flat out.

At least partial confirmation was provided in 1976 by classic Chevy dealer Bob Wingate and his unrestored 283-bhp Bel Air Sport Coupe. With close-ratio column-shift three-speed, 3.70:1 rear axle, and less than 30,000 original miles, it was a scorcher. Though Wingate didn't time 0-60-mph acceleration, he did make four standing quarter-mile runs at Southern California's Irwindale Raceway. The results speak for themselves: 14.88 seconds at 103.86 mph, two identical runs at 14.75 seconds/103.6 mph, and 14.21 seconds at 104.01 mph—all in strictly stock trim! In fact, he even ran with the air cleaner and street tires. Fuel economy seems academic in this context, but Wingate reported 20.8 mpg—on high test gas, naturally—including travel to and from the track. "That figure, too, says an awful lot for fuel

Interior Color and Trim Selections for the 1957 Chevrolet

BEL AIR MODELS

Convertible

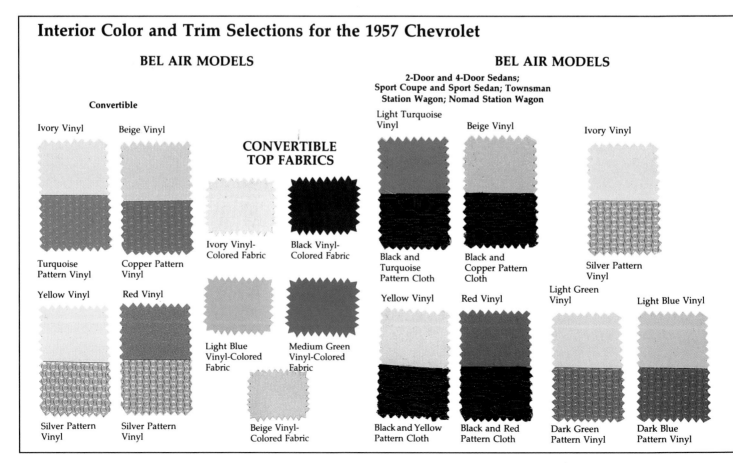

Ivory Vinyl

Beige Vinyl

Turquoise Pattern Vinyl

Copper Pattern Vinyl

Yellow Vinyl

Red Vinyl

Silver Pattern Vinyl

Silver Pattern Vinyl

CONVERTIBLE TOP FABRICS

Ivory Vinyl-Colored Fabric

Black Vinyl-Colored Fabric

Light Blue Vinyl-Colored Fabric

Medium Green Vinyl-Colored Fabric

Beige Vinyl-Colored Fabric

BEL AIR MODELS

2-Door and 4-Door Sedans; Sport Coupe and Sport Sedan; Townsman Station Wagon; Nomad Station Wagon

Light Turquoise Vinyl

Beige Vinyl

Ivory Vinyl

Black and Turquoise Pattern Cloth

Black and Copper Pattern Cloth

Silver Pattern Vinyl

Yellow Vinyl

Red Vinyl

Light Green Vinyl

Light Blue Vinyl

Black and Yellow Pattern Cloth

Black and Red Pattern Cloth

Dark Green Pattern Vinyl

Dark Blue Pattern Vinyl

injection," he wrote, "because the twin four-barrel setups I've owned have always been pretty thirsty."

A major engineering development is never simple—or easy—and though Ramjet was a milestone in Chevy's brief performance history, bugs were inevitable. Aside from its sheer complexity, Vince Piggins noted that the injectors were "very prone to dirt, clogging, dirty fuel, and what not." Initially, they also absorbed enough heat to cause rough idling, later cured by extending them further into the air stream. Yet despite such teething troubles and slow public acceptance, Ramjet was soon developed to the point that it would continue as a Corvette option all the way

(continued on page 89)

The Bel Air Nomad was in its final year as a specialty station wagon model in 1957, though the name would be transferred to top-line conventional wagons in 1958. As in 1955 and '56, it was both the priciest and rarest of all Chevrolets. It retailed for $2757, and only 6103 were built for the '57 model year. The Nomad was probably a losing proposition for Chevy because so many body and trim parts were unique to it, particularly at the rear. Since only 22,375 Nomads were built during its three-year run, it's likely that not enough were sold to pay for its tooling costs. (Owner: Bill Bodnarchuk)

BEL AIR MODELS	**TWO-TEN MODELS** 2-Door Sedan, 4-Door Sedan, Sport Coupe, Sport Sedan	**TWO-TEN MODELS** Two-Ten Delray Club Coupe	**ONE-FIFTY MODELS** 2-Door Sedan, 4-Door Sedan, Utility Sedan
Silver Vinyl	Ivory Vinyl	Ivory Vinyl	Black Vinyl
Black and Silver Pattern Cloth	Charcoal Pattern Cloth	Charcoal Pattern Vinyl	Black and Gray Pattern Cloth

Handyman Station Wagon

Light Green Vinyl	Light Blue Vinyl	Light Green Vinyl	Light Blue Vinyl	Light Green Vinyl	Beige Vinyl	Black Vinyl	Dark Green Vinyl
Black and Green Pattern Cloth	Black and Blue Pattern Cloth	Dark Green Pattern Cloth	Dark Blue Pattern Cloth	Dark Green Pattern Vinyl	Copper Pattern Vinyl	Black and Gray Pattern Vinyl	Green and Gray Pattern Vinyl

85

The '57 Chevrolet, here a Bel Air Sport Coupe (*right*), featured a massive-looking bumper-grille ensemble highlighted by a "floating" horizontal bar housing the parking lights and Chevy crest. Note the twin "windsplits" on the hood. The rear (*top*) featured modest fins and low-riding taillights. The instrument panel (*above*), new for 1957, was dubbed the "Command Post," and sometimes referred to as a "Flight Panel." (Car courtesy of Sunshine Auto Center)

The 1957 Chevy Bel Air Sport Coupe is seen here in Colonial Cream, a slightly more subdued yellow than the Harvest Gold and Crocus Yellow of 1955-56. Ever striving for a "rich" Cadillac look, Chevy treated the Bel Air to gold trim on the grille mesh, front and rear nameplates and "V," and on the front fender "hashmarks." (Owner: Bill Goodsene)

through 1965.

And it served Chevy well during the 1957 racing season. In late 1956, an "independent engineering firm" called Southern Engineering Development Company (SEDCO) was formed with tacit division assistance and Vince Piggins in charge. It duly prepared a squadron of cars for the Daytona Speed Weeks in February, to be shepherded by Piggins and team manager Dick Rathmann.

They did well, to say the least. Chevy finished the two-way flying mile 1-2-3 in Class 4 (213-259 cid), the top car averaging 102.157 miles per hour. A Ford was fourth—seven seconds slower over the distance. In Class 5 (259-305 cid) that same day, Chevy took the first 33 places in a field of 37, with Paul Goldsmith fastest at 131.076 mph. Two days later, Chevy was again 1-2-3 in competition for automatic/four-barrel cars, the best being Al Simonsen's 118.460 mph. Chevy also dominated Class 5 standing-mile acceleration by finishing 1-18, the last car 10 seconds ahead of the top-place Ford, which came in 19th. In all, Chevy scored a convincing 574 points to win the Pure Oil Manufacturer's Trophy, clobbering runner-up Ford (309) and third-place Mercury (174).

Then, a setback. While Chevy romped at Daytona, the Automobile Manufacturers Association (AMA) met in Detroit at the behest of the National Safety Council, the

AAA (by now out of racing), and several of its own members, who insisted that the "horsepower race" and the competition emphasis in auto advertising were breeding a generation of dangerous, accident-prone drivers. Accordingly, a resolution was prepared recommending that automakers henceforth not participate in racing, supply pace cars, or publicize race results. The resolution passed unanimously in June 1957. But this oft-called "ban" produced only a temporary lull. Ford and Chrysler were battling openly again by the early Sixties, and GM hadn't really stopped, providing under-the-table support while publicly declaring that it "wasn't in racing."

So Chevy never left the dragstrips or the stock-car tracks. In fact, on Labor Day '57, three months *after* the AMA edict, Speedy Thompson averaged 100 mph to win the NASCAR Southern 500 at Darlington. Piggins' racing parts business flourished from continuing demand for heavy-duty "export" components, and Chevys kept on winning in '58. A highlight was another Southern 500 victory, this time by Fireball Roberts, who averaged 102.6 mph in his '57. (Chevy won again the following year, with Jim Reed in a '59 model.)

Which brings up an interesting postscript. Right after the AMA decision, Piggins issued a sought-after booklet, the "1957 Chevrolet Stock Car Competition Guide," with everything a would-be Chevy

racer needed to know: heavy-duty equipment, body modifications, track chassis set-ups, competition tuning, spare parts, even how to register a race car, including addresses. This and more clandestine factory support contributed to a steady stream of competitive, often formidable Chevrolet stockers. By 1961, when the next generation of high-performance street

Chevys was born, "USA-1" was number one with hundreds of racers, amateur and professional. The staid, pre-1955 image was gone forever.

And with model year 1958, so were the "classic" Chevys. Ironically, the division had been looking upmarket since the first of this memorable breed, the '55, and its aspirations were now realized in the biggest,

Opposite page: Tropical Turquoise was a popular color on Chevys in 1957, and it looked particularly good on the Bel Air convertible, which can be seen here in both top-up and top-down form. *This page:* The "budget-basement" '57 Chevy was the One-Ten Utility Sedan (*top*), which had a platform in place of a rear seat. At $1885, it undercut the One-Ten two-door by $111. The least expensive wagon was the two-door six-passenger One-Fifty Handyman: $2307.

Despite a production run of only 20 in 1956, the El Morocco (*both pages*) reappeared for 1957, looking even more like a Cadillac Eldorado. It copped its "shark" fins and single headlights from the Biarritz/Seville, the L-shaped bodyside moldings and broad appliqués on the lower rear-quarters from the $13,000 Eldorado Brougham. The dashboard plaque even read "El Morocco Brougham." Only 16 were built for 1957. (Owner: Charles Davis)

heaviest, most powerful Chevrolets ever. Symbolic of the new order was the Bel Air Impala, a lush convertible and Sport Coupe with Cadillac looks and luxury to match, and a four-door successor to the handsome Nomad, identical with other Bel Air wagons except for its tailgate "bananas."

Enthusiasts have long condemned the '58s as the first of the larger and clumsier standard Chevrolets that would persist through the mid-Seventies. Today we can view them more kindly: right for their day, superior to most Detroit contemporaries— and the start of a successful new chapter in Chevrolet history.

Of course, opening one chapter means closing another, and car lovers everywhere have long mourned the loss of the "classic" Chevys. But thank goodness for the memories: of powerful performance and elegant engineering, nostalgic styling and raw stamina, high popularity and historic impact.

Come to think of it, these great cars are still making memories. And that's why they always will.

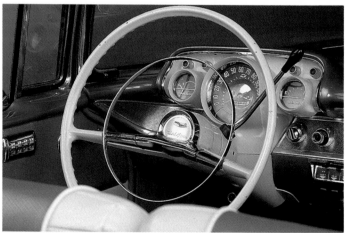

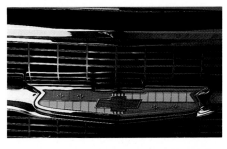

Opposite page: Chevy V-8s for 1957 included the 162-horsepower 265 with two-barrel carburetor (*top left*), 220-horsepower 283 with a four-barrel carb (*center left*), and the 250/283-horsepower 283 with Ramjet fuel injection (*bottom left*). Various interior color and trim selections were available; this Bel Air Sport Coupe featured bench seats upholstered in red vinyl and black and red pattern cloth (*top right*). The "Command Post" dashboard placed a large speedometer directly ahead of the driver (*center right*); it was flanked by a smaller temperature gauge on the left and gasoline gauge on the right. A Bel Air badge was placed between the radio and clock (*center bottom*). *This page*: A smattering of the many '57 Chevrolet accessories available, as well as the "Body by Fisher" plaque, which was located on the step-plate, and the Chevy crest, which was found on the grille bar.

1957 Accessories

Air conditioning
Electric fender antenna
Manual fender antenna, left and right
Autronic Eye headlamp control
Front and rear basket units
Seatbelts
Wiring junction block
Safetylight bracket
Power brakes
Locking gas cap
Continental wheel carrier
Electric clock
Compass
Full wheel covers
Bumper cushion
Tissue dispenser
Gasoline filter unit
License plate frame (chrome or gold)
Glareshades
Tinted safety glass
Bumper guards
Door edge guards
Shoulder harness
Heater and defroster
Horn with third note
Tool kit
Kool Kooshion
Back-up lamps
Courtesy lamps

Cigarette lighter
Floor mats
Outside rearview mirrors
Inside non-glare rearview mirror
Vanity visor mirror
Body sill moulding
Lower trunk lid edge moulding
Radio: manual, push-button, or Wonder Bar
Armrests
Safetylight with mirror
Radiator insect screen
Power-positioned front seat
Electric shaver
Door handle shields
Parking brake signal
Rear seat speaker
Wheel spinners
Hand portable spotlight
Power steering
Vacuum tank
Whitewall tires
Ventshades
Traffic light viewer
Outside visors
Inside visors
Windshield washer (push-button or foot-operated)
Electric-power window lifts
Electric windshield wipers

Of the three "classic" Chevys, most people seem to favor the '57, and among the '57s the Bel Air convertible reigns supreme. With its new 283 V-8, the '57 was the fastest of the 1955-57 generation, and its styling still strikes a responsive chord with millions of people. Perhaps Chevy said it best way back in 1957 when it claimed that "It's sweet, smooth and sassy with new velvety V8 power, new roadability, a new ride and everything it takes to make you the relaxed master of any road you travel." Perhaps that's *still* true!

1957 Chevrolet Specifications, Prices, and Production

Model	Overall Length	Curb Weight	List Price	Production
1957 (115-inch wheelbase)				
ONE-FIFTY				
1502 Sedan, two-door	200.0	3,211	1,996	70,774
1503 Sedan, four-door	200.0	3,236	2,048	52,266
1512 Sedan, utility	200.0	3,163	1,885	8,300
1529 Handyman, two-door wagon	200.0	3,406	2,307	14,740
TWO-TEN				
2102 Sedan, two-door	200.0	3,225	2,122	162,090
2103 Sedan, four-door	200.0	3,270	2,174	260,401
2109 Townsman, four-door wagon	200.0	3,461	2,456	127,803
2113 Sport Sedan, four-door hardtop	200.0	3,320	2,270	16,178
2119 Beauville, four-door wagon	200.0	3,561	2,563	21,083
2124 Delray, coupe	200.0	3,220	2,162	25,644
2129 Handyman, two-door wagon	200.0	3,406	2,402	17,528
2154 Sport Coupe, hardtop	200.0	3,260	2,204	22,631
BEL AIR				
2402 Sedan, two-door	200.0	3,232	2,238	62,751
2403 Sedan, four-door	200.0	3,276	2,290	254,331
2409 Townsman, four-door wagon	200.0	3,460	2,580	27,375
2413 Sport Sedan, hardtop	200.0	3,340	2,364	137,672
2429 Nomad, two-door wagon	200.0	3,465	2,757	6,103
2434 Convertible, coupe	200.0	3,409	2,511	47,562
2454 Sport Coupe, hardtop	200.0	3,278	2,299	166,426

Engine/Transmission Availability

	cid	bore/stroke (inches)	compression ratio	bhp @ rpm	carb	trans
1957						
Six	235	3.56 × 3.94	8.00:1	140 @ 4200	1V	3-sp., OD, PG[1]
V-8	265	3.75 × 3.00	8.00:1	162 @ 4400	2V	3-sp., OD
V-8	283	3.88 × 3.00	8.50:1	185 @ 4600	2V	PG[1], TG[2]
V-8	283	3.88 × 3.00	9.50:1	220 @ 4800	4V	3-sp., OD, PG[1], TG[2]
V-8	283	3.88 × 3.00	9.50:1	245 @ 5000	2-4V	3-sp.[3], PG[1], TG[2]
V-8	283	3.88 × 3.00	9.50:1	250 @ 5000	FI[4]	3-sp.[3], PG[1], TG[2]
V-8	283	3.88 × 3.00	9.50:1	270 @ 6000	2-4V	3-sp.[3]
V-8	283	3.88 × 3.00	10.50:1	283 @ 6200	FI[4]	3-sp.[3]

[1]Powerglide   [2]Turboglide   [3]Close-ratio three speed   [4]Fuel Injection